MW00399483

The Elhardt Family Guide to Your First Rental Property

By
Brian A. Elhardt

DISCLAIMER:

This book is our true story about our journey in long-distance rental real estate investing. In this book we share exactly what we did, how we did it, and the exact tools we used. Some tools cost money, and some are free. This book does not contain all information available on the subject of real estate investing. This book is not intended in any way to be legal, tax, or financial advice for you and your particular situation. We cannot advise what is best for you, nor can we take responsibility in any way for your results. We are not an attorney, CPA, financial advisor, or debt counselor. If you have the need for expert advice from such professionals, consult with the appropriate practitioner. At any time in the book when we say "we can" or "you should" or similar language it is simply a manner of speaking and not advice based on analysis of your individual situation. Every effort has been made to supply accurate information in this book, but there is always the possibility of content errors, typographical errors, or information becoming obsolete with the passing of time. By reading this book you agree that you will have no recourse against the author or Family Wealth Traditions, Inc. in any way for any injury resulting from, or alleged to be resulting from following in my footsteps of real estate investing, or any information provided in this book. You hereby agree to be bound by this Disclaimer, or you may cease reading this book now, and immediately return it within the guarantee time for a full refund.

All of this being said, rental real estate investing is one of the most intuitive, user-friendly ways to invest that exists, and being educated, as well as finding the right professionals within real estate to guide you, can greatly minimize potential risk. I hope that personalizing the journey to real estate investing by reading our story will inspire you, which is the sole purpose of this book.

Copyright © 2020 Family Wealth Traditions, Inc.

All rights reserved. No part of this book may be reproduced in any form without permission in writing from the publisher. Amazon Edition 3.0

www.ElhardtRealEstate.com

Contents

Preface

It was the summer of 1984, and as an 11-year-old boy I was sent up to spend the summer with my aunt in Redding, California. Redding was a very small town compared to my hometown of Los Angeles, but it was surrounded by a lot more nature, and so I suppose my mother saw it as a cheap version of summer camp for me.

My aunt was actually my grandfather's sister (so perhaps I should call her my great-aunt?). I had never met my grandfather as he died before I was born (yet my mother would always say how much I reminded her of him - which never meant anything to me at the time).

Anyway, on top of all of the fun things an 11-year-old usually does on summer vacation with his friends, the Summer Olympics had also just been held in Los Angeles, and I was still on an unbelievable high from that. By contrast, this slow town, with no friends and my "old" aunt, was a terribly boring change of pace.

My aunt, who was old, now lived alone (I think she had been married a long time ago but he died? Not sure...) and had no kids. She was "retired" (but I didn't know from what) and had all day to do as she pleased. Unfortunately, what pleased her to do was some pretty boring stuff, and I got to tag along.

My aunt attended a church that was literally across the street from her house, and had few friends except for her best friend Marie. She liked to pray the Rosary, and tend to her rose garden, which she would water endlessly. She drove a Chrysler K-Car, which if you don't know, was the ultimate boxy, boring car a 5-year-old draws out of instinct when you hand them a crayon and ask them to draw a car.

Having no concept of how to entertain an 11-year-old boy, my aunt bought me a used bicycle, and encouraged me to go exploring the neighborhood. An exhaustive tour took up about 20 minutes of the 13-hour summer daylight. Combine my daily bike tour with a whopping 3 channels of re-runs coming through clearly on her TV's rabbit-ear antennas, and there was my excitement for the day. Fortunately, my extreme boredom soon gave way to ingenuity of sorts. I decided I would start a business "restoring" bicycles.

My business plan essentially consisted of me buying literally a $5 or $10 bicycle out of the Penny Saver (before Craigslist existed). I would then buy a can of spray paint in any color that stuck me, usually blue or silver. Then I would go to an actual bike shop and spend no more than a dollar or two on some stickers that belonged on much more expensive bicycles that have no relation whatsoever to the no-name piece of junk I just bought.

Once I had all of my "restoration" supplies back home, I would take the wheels off the project/victim bike and then take the rest of it and either lay it down directly on the back lawn, or lean it up against a shrub, and start spray painting everything in sight – chain, sprocket, you name it (there were blue marks on the back hedge the rest of the summer). About 20 minutes later when the paint was dry (which I could tell because lawn clippings weren't sticking to it any more) I would slap on the stickers and put the wheels back. Bam! New bike! I was so proud of my work, I even proudly took some before-and-after photos, as if somehow I had made the bikes *better!*

After restoration, the next step was to put the "new" franken-bike back in the same Penny Saver, for 5 bucks more and see who called. I remember selling one for $10 to a kid in the neighborhood. It was silver, and I was especially proud of my sticker job on that one. You see, I had blessed that particular no-name bike with stickers from *several* great bike brands, (I figured somehow their power would seep into this bike). I'll never forget that just a few hours after it had been sold, the kid's dad actually brought the bike back for a refund! Imagine a $10 bike being so bad you actually want a refund! I mean, what's it worth just as scrap metal? My aunt mumbled some words to him in my defense as she returned his money…I hid inside. That was the end of my bike business.

The single-most exciting day of the summer was one day when my aunt got a call from someone about mid-morning. The phone never rang so that alone was amazing (and a bit startling as the ringer was on its loudest setting due to my aunt's hearing problem).

The conversation she had with the caller was very short, and I member her saying something like "Ok, I figure it's about time anyway." I had no idea what they were talking about, all I know is that as soon as she hung up we had to immediately pile in the car and go to Sears. She had clip-on sunglasses that fit over her prescription glasses, and when they got clipped on, I knew it was time for action! Of course, "action" usually meant some boring errand, but hey, it was something! Compared to what else we had going on that day (nothing) I felt like Batman and Robin springing into action to go to a crime scene.

Arriving at Sears, she promptly headed for a department I had never been in before. Without hesitation, my aunt told the salesman that she needed to purchase a Swamp Cooler (which turns out later was a primitive form of air conditioning) and have it installed at such and such address (not her house). The item cost $500, which she paid for in cash. I had never seen that much money before in my life. I will never forget feeling like I had just witnessed the richest person in the world transact a magical purchase of a mystical item destined for a different dimension. I asked what all of this magic was about, and she said not to worry about it, so I didn't.

The only other "interesting" days that summer were once a month when my aunt had several visitors that would stop by the house. The visitors were regular looking people of middle age, and there were maybe 4 or 5 of them tops. They would arrive at various times throughout the day, and stay just for a moment to give my aunt an envelope. My aunt would chat with them briefly while she held open the screen door, and then they went on their way for another month. My aunt was very secretive, unfortunately, so the summer would end without my gaining much knowledge about what a swamp cooler was, or what was in those envelopes.

At long last, the horrid, hot, boring summer of '84 was over. I left my franken-bike masterpieces behind and returned to what was by contrast, my jet-set-paced life of Los Angeles. I was glad to be reunited with my real friends, my real TV, and my real bicycle. I even looked forward to school, if you can believe it.

Years went by, and eventually my aunt suffered a stroke. My mother went up north to handle her affairs, which included selling "a couple of houses" my aunt had to pay for her care. Soon after, my aunt passed away, and my normal life as an adult began. By "normal," of course, I mean to get a job, pay bills, rack up debt, and wonder why I never have any time. I had a 401(k), but without much in it. I looked around and everyone was in the same boat.

While I plodded along in my young adulthood on a normal job-track, my entrepreneurial instincts from my bicycle business were still lurking dormant inside me. I started to pick up books on investing, money, and business to study what the rich did that I (and seemingly everyone else) did not. In the course of this study, but unfortunately after my aunt's death, I was able to finally put 2 and 2 together about everything I had seen in the summer of '84. I was finally able to see my aunt's life for what it really was. When I did, it hit me like a ton of bricks as tear-jerking memories of boredom from that summer faded to the miracles that had taken place before my eyes.

That summer in my youth, my aunt wasn't "retired" from anything – she was still "working" the career she had been in for decades. My aunt wasn't bored, she was *free*. My aunt's life wasn't mundane; it was *peaceful* as she chose it. My aunt wasn't rich – she had *cash flow*. My aunt wasn't a "little old land-lady." My aunt was a financially independent *real estate investor*. The monthly guests at her screen door were her tenants paying rent! Her business partner was her brother - my grandfather (the one I reminded my mother of) - and watching her those many years ago was ultimately a prelude to what was literally in my blood: a passion and purpose for investing in and teaching real estate today.

My Great Aunt, Laura C. Rowley, and her Brother and Business Partner, my Grandfather, Leonard G. Elhardt

Dedication

This book is dedicated to you - a serious person willing to pick up a book and get closer to their dream of investing in rental real estate, but that has never actually done it. Maybe you've read books, gone to seminars, and talked about investing for years - but something has stopped you.

Perhaps what has stopped you are horror stories from amateurs about the pitfalls of being a landlord (toilets breaking in the middle of the night is the most common "ghost story" told...lol).

Perhaps what has stopped you are investing gurus that have scared you through their advanced strategies that seem way over your head. Maybe you don't trust yourself to even know what a good deal looks like - or, you simply do not live in a part of the country where the numbers work well for rentals, and the thought of investing long distance freaks you out.

Perhaps you are simply surrounded by traditionally-minded people living typical financial lives and the thought of doing something no one else you personally know is doing simply sounds lonely and scary, and you don't know where to begin.

Whatever the reason that has stopped you, I hear you, and I have good news for you. I remember what it was like to feel that way, and I know what you really need to learn to get started. I've already spent the thousands of dollars learning and doing deals the guru-way so you don't have to – and want to know something? Nothing they teach is as powerful, simple, or gives more peace than rental property done the way you will be taught here: Aunt Laura's way...our way...and you are more prepared than you think.

So, buckle up, take my hand, and let's begin...

Brian Elhardt, *2020*

Introduction

As a mental-primer to the information in this book, let's briefly consider the topic of financial freedom…When, exactly, are you financially free? When you have a million dollars? When you hit a certain age?

No… You are financially free - by absolute definition - when your *monthly passive income* (income you do not have to go to a job to get) equals your *monthly expenses*.

Think about it - if you need $5,000 a month to pay your bills, and $5,000 a month comes to you out of a "magic wallet" - or from rental income - you are free. Now, no one with $5,000 of income would ever be called rich - but with an endless fountain of that income - that you do not have to go work a job for - you are *free*. Consider my story about Aunt Laura in the preface of this book.

Nothing known to mankind produces this passive income better, faster, or is more historically tried-and-true in doing so - than is rental real estate. This has been true since the night of the birth of Jesus, when Joseph and Mary were in search of someone to pay for the use their real estate to sleep in for the night. Nothing has ever changed about that.

If you want freedom, why do you want it? What would you do with your time you now cannot? Emotionalize that feeling - this will serve as your motivation - your "why" that will make the process ahead of you worth the effort.

So, with your deepest dreams fully in mind – let us begin.

PART 1

WHY RENTAL REAL ESTATE

Chapter 1:

Why Rental Real Estate?

As we begin, I wanted to make something perfectly clear: When most people hear about the general term "Real Estate Investing," they naturally think of people trying to "fix and flip" a property for a quick profit as has been the subject of many popular reality TV shows. Or, perhaps someone thinks of buying and holding onto a property for market appreciation over time, selling it for a profit one day far into the future. For those type of investors, they are looking for large chunks of money all at once by "buying low, selling high," (also called "Capital Gain" investing).

These "investors" are actually what I call "house dealers." No, not like drug dealers, (lol) but, yes, exactly like car dealers or antique dealers. They are looking to buy something cheap, shine it up, and sell it for a profit. There is nothing wrong with this business model, but I need to make it clear that this is not what we're talking about in rental real estate. House dealing will never set you free - it is a job, a business, that can absolutely make you a lot of money, but once you sell one house you must now go off to sell the next, forever. This is *not* how Aunt Laura was free to water her roses all day.

Our objective in Rental Real Estate Investing is the complete opposite: We are looking to create a strong, consistent stream of rental income - beginning now, and lasting into the future for decades, maybe even forever (also called "Cash-Flow" investing). Our focus on Cash-Flow allows us to avoid hasty, panic decisions in acquiring a property, and also to all but ignore the long-term market price fluctuations or appreciation of a property.

As a comparison from elsewhere in life: we are not looking to grow a tree and cut it down to sell as lumber, we are looking to take care of it and harvest its fruit year after year. It sounds slow, steady, and boring, and it is, that's why they don't make TV shows about Rental Real Estate! But it is also why little old "church ladies" like my Aunt Laura can build freedom with it.

So, with that in mind, let us take a closer look at the wonderful benefits of Rental Real Estate - which will be discussed thoroughly later - they include:

A Calm, Cash-Flow Focus

As stated above, but to reiterate again - other common forms of investing, such as the stock market, are "Capital Gain" focused - meaning, you need to "buy low and sell high." This is also the case with "house flipping." On the other hand, as rental real-estate investors, we are looking for the ongoing income that our properties produce. Month after month, year after year, decade after decade, rent keeps pouring in - *even if there are times the actual value of the property itself may dip*. This allows us to really take our time and calmly think about the property we acquire.

Low Risk & Practicality

Unlike the typical wisdom of "higher risk brings higher return," as we will see more vividly later, rental real estate can bring impressive returns on a slow, calm basis. Of course, you need to know what you are doing for this to be the case, but that is no different than driving a car. Once you learn how to drive, you may not be a race-car driver, or you may not even want to drive on the freeway - but you most certainly can drive safely around the block. Well, rental real estate is the "driving around the block" of real estate investing, and it is all we are going to be doing here to build a great rental income business for you.

You Never Really Spend the Money

One of the most glorious aspects of rental real estate is that from a practical perspective, when you buy rental real estate, you really never spend the money - you are just moving your cash into another asset class. By purchasing rental real estate, you are literally converting your money into something not only of value, but of *usefulness*. A house isn't just a commodity like gold that sits there and can go up in value, it's an actual, functional, physical place, where people can live, (and heck, where even you could live if you had to, or wanted to).

Contrast this with what happens when you start most businesses where you actually do spend money you will never see again - on rent, on payroll, etc. If the business fails, that money you invested is really gone. How many people have literally invested their life savings in a restaurant, retail store, or other business that didn't work and they really did lose everything? With rental real estate, however, if your plan to use a property as a rental investment somehow completely fails, the worst that happens is that you are left with an actual physical place people can live in that you can sell to someone else, or use yourself. Whenever you may wish to convert your real estate back into cash – you can call your Realtor and just sell it. Whether the value at that point has gone up or down – you still own an asset that is worth something.

True Investment Asset Diversification

Traditional investment advisors teach the benefits of "diversifying your portfolio" and "not putting all of your eggs all in one basket." But then they go on to sell you stocks, bonds, and mutual funds, all of which are in the same asset class! ("Paper" assets). That's like selling you different seats on the same bus! However, when you purchase a piece of physical, rental real estate, now you have truly diversified into something unrelated to the returns in any other asset class. If the stock market goes up or down this month, people still need to pay their rent.

Risk Management

If your property burns down, or washes away in a flood, or someone slips and hurts themselves, your insurance policies should cover it. If you get a terrible tenant, you can pay a few hundred dollars to an attorney and evict them. If aliens from Mars beam your property up into their mother-ship and insurance won't cover it - the vacant dirt lot under the property is still worth something...lol. While not ideal, knowing these recoverable events are all the "worst case scenarios" is very reassuring. Contrast this with the stock market tanking while all you can do is sit and watch the news.

Control of Outcome

Unlike the stock market, rental real estate allows us to calmly look at the returns a property will be producing *before* - not *after* - you make the purchase. The property price and market rent you can expect as income is known up front, and is *not* based on speculation or wishful thinking. This alone is so different than a typical stock market investment I almost want to call for a moment of silence to really digest it...you know your returns on investment *before* you invest. (This will become clearer as we discuss property analysis later).

Leverage

Leverage is just a fancy term for the fact that the bank will give you a mortgage for most of the money you'll need to buy rental real estate! Just as a crow-bar can give you the leverage to move an object you could not otherwise move on your own physical strength - the leverage of being able to borrow most of your purchase money will allow you to obtain properties you could not have afforded on your own financial strength. A bank is willing to partner with you by loaning you most of the purchase price of just about any rental real estate you might be looking to buy. Yet, any profit is yours to keep. That's using the power of "OPM" (Other People's Money) - also called Leverage.

Multiple Profit Centers

While the income produced from your tenants paying rent is the most obvious source of profit from rental real estate, there are actually three potential sources of income, which are:

1. **Rental Income**: The cash-flow left over from your tenant's rent payment, after you pay all expenses. This is the first and most obvious profit we make as rental real estate investors.

2. **Mortgage Pay-Down**: From the rent we receive from our tenants, of course we must first pay the expenses associated with owning any property. This includes insurance, property tax, and yes, your mortgage payment. But a part of the mortgage payment

is actually yours to keep. Consider this: part of every mortgage payment is interest, and part is principal being paid off, lowering the balance on your mortgage.

Lowering the balance on your mortgage increases the equity in your rental property. Since it is the rent received from your tenant being used to make your mortgage payment, your tenant is literally slowly paying off your property for you! While it is not liquid cash to spend today, the equity being built through your mortgage being paid-down is yours to count as internal profit (more on this later as we cover rental property analysis).

3. **Appreciation**: As rental investors, we never want to count on the value of our properties to rise to make a profit, that is pure speculation and purchasing a property on "hope" sabotages the inherent safety of rental property. However, over time, the elements that make a city a great place for a rental property may also quite possibly cause the value of your properties to increase with the passage of time. If nothing else, simple inflation may do this for us as well.

When our properties do increase in value, we have that increased equity as profit for our use. To access this equity, we can choose to refinance the property with cash-out, or, sell the property (possibly to roll into the purchase of an even larger rental property). In this regard, Appreciation is a nice bonus - but again - a rental property you are looking to purchase must stand on its own performance from a cash-flow perspective to pass the test we will be teaching.

4. Tax Benefits

Rental real estate is unique in that, for tax purposes, it is treated more like a business rather than a typical investment (such as a mutual fund). When you have a rental property, you effectively have a business - even if that business is renting one property to one person. As a real business, you have access to all of the tax write-offs of any other business owner. If you need to travel, purchase supplies, maintain a home office, have a phone line, etc., to run that business, there is a strong possibility these expenses will be tax deductible. You can even form a legal entity like an LLC to specifically hold and run your property.

Also, and this is big, the IRS looks at a property like a huge piece of equipment (like a restaurant's refrigerator or a farmer's tractor) that *depreciates* in value as its usable life goes on and it "wears out." This, even if in reality - unlike the tractor, the value of your real estate may actually be *increasing*. Yes, that is not a misprint.

(You will be discussing these concepts and much more with the real-estate-savvy CPA you will absolutely have to have on your team which we will discuss later).

Quadrant of the 4 Profit-Centers of Rental Real-Estate:

RENTAL CASH-FLOW	MARKET VALUE APPRECIATION
MORTGAGE PAY-DOWN	DEPRECIATION & TAX BENEFITS

Intuitive Simplicity

Unlike other types of investing that require special education, or "investment experts" to guide you, Rental Real Estate is extremely intuitive and easy to learn. That is because since the day we were born we have lived inside some sort of real estate, so we are extremely familiar with at least the physical aspects of it. You already know what a property looks like and feels like that you would want to live in for a given price.

You even already understand some fundamental financial aspects of real estate. You know that most real estate has to be paid for every month, either through rent or a mortgage. In fact, I think most people are already programmed with that is needed to be great rental real estate investors, they just don't know it yet.

That being said, there is definitely a science to apply to the art of investing in rental real estate that is well worth learning. Two properties can be side by side and through analysis (which we will cover later) one can offer a great rental investment opportunity while the other does not.

I firmly believe that if you can graduate high school, with all of the Algebra, French Poetry, and other impractical caca-poo-poo we were all forced to learn - you certainly have the raw aptitude for what we will teach you in analyzing rental real estate. (My apologies to Algebra teachers and French poets - however, you French Algebra teachers - you're on your own).

A word of caution here, however - more than analysis, the other things you'll need for successful real estate investing will include some people skills in building relationships with your team (as we will discuss). The last ingredient will simply be your determination to actually take action. You may analyze that a pool of water isn't deep enough to drown in - but you still have to decide to avoid "analysis paralysis" and just jump in! What you learn by analyzing, but then taking action, will develop your gut for investing that you'll learn to trust as you gain experience.

A Slow Pace

It is not uncommon for the stock market to have single days when the market can drop 500, or even 1,000 points. But in real estate, even in a housing "crash" this will never happen to you in a day. Real Estate takes weeks, months and years to do what it's going to do price-wise. You will never be on a frantic call to your "house broker" yelling "sell sell sell!" before today's closing bell. That's not just the nature of real estate. If a neighborhood is trending toward getting better or worse, or if real estate prices are trending toward higher or lower, that all takes time. You are absolutely going to have a chance to take a look, do some analysis, and make a calm decision about moves you may wish to make.

Consistent Returns

What can be surprising to learn is that rental rates have little to do with underlying property price changes. If the price of your property dips, or surges, in a relatively short period of time, that will most likely not affect your rent - which typically slowly rises with inflation like the cost of milk, furniture, or anything else. In fact, in times when it is difficult for people to purchase homes, rental prices can actually go up! That's a major point to understand because it can be easy to think that property prices and rental rates are locked together – and they are not. Rental rates are connected with inflation, and with people's desire and ability to pay. If jobs are heading into a community and so people both want to, and are able to, rent homes there – then the rents will rise. (How to pick a good area for rental homes will be discussed much more later).

It Matters to the Community

As the owner of a rental property, you are literally a business owner providing a service to customers in your community. I don't know about you - but what makes a community a great place to live isn't usually the rocks and the trees - it's the people, and businesses built by owners who really care that make up the experience of a community. That's you now. Someone is going to have a professional experience with the home they rent thanks to you. That matters. We've had a tenant tell us about how wonderful it is that we fix anything that goes wrong with the house right away because their last landlord didn't care. She's a working mom trying to get her kids to bed - not trying to make the furnace work.

There is no more intimate of a product to "sell" than where someone lives. Someone's phone, car, or shoes, do not affect everything in someone's life, but, where they live does, literally. Being a professional rental property owner instead of an amateur hack makes a huge difference in people's lives. In my youth, I was a renter for many years. While I hope everyone owns real estate eventually in their life, providing a service to those in the renting-stage of their life has value and honor in it, and you can make someone's life infinitely easier or harder by what kind of experience you give them as your tenant. Provide excellence and expect the same in return. Be a true professional, and keep both tenants happy and your business thriving my attending both to the human-side and numbers-side of the business.

Timelessness

Unlike a fashion that can be "trendy" or a technology that can become obsolete - human beings will always need a place to live and someone to pay to live in that place.
The analysis of what an opportunity for a great rental property looks like on paper will *not* change with time - but where those opportunities can be found geographically just might.

The concepts and processes taught in this book will remain timeless, as they were for Aunt Laura, as they are for me, as they are for you. But, the specific numbers, interest rates, and city examples I will give within this book will be out of date almost immediately. In that way, consider this book a "cook book" of sorts. The ingredients of a great investment are the same – but where those ingredients can be found today – in your life, right now, in real-time, will always be changing, that's why your role as an investor will always be needed.

But don't worry – there will always be gold to be found. The Elhardt Family investing legacy has already followed the vein of gold from California to Indiana. Where is it heading next? This book is your compass…the examples are conceptual – but your adventure will be in your own time with your own team.

Legacy

Because of the timelessness and simplicity of rental real estate, it is not only easy and relevant to learn - it is easy and endlessly relevant to teach. Most especially, to teach your next generation. Rental real estate - both the education and the properties themselves - can be a torch passed from one generation to another easier than any other business/investment one can imagine. So long as the next generation is taught both the mentality of stewardship, and the basic skills of investing, there is no reason why your family's wealth can't grow from one generation to another. Part of my Aunt Laura's portfolio has touched three generations so far.

After your lifetime of successful investing, you will have properties to pass down to your children – so they will have hard assets to start with. But, much more importantly, with the timeless knowledge you also pass down, your children will have the wisdom to keep, or re-deploy those assets in ways that are more in alignment with the unchanging fundamentals of investing as they manifest in their future time.

My fingers tremble a bit and my eyes water as I type this paragraph as I sense future generations of our own family reading this book long after we have gone on to join Laura and Len in the cheerleading section of Heaven. I have no doubt you will be the ones to write future revisions to this book as timeless truths blend with timely tips of your wisdom.

Passive by Nature

It will take time and effort to obtain and establish a good rental property - but once it is up and running, it largely runs without you. What time it will take can easily be found outside of normal working hours - so, you will not have to quit your job to acquire rental real estate. Rental Real Estate generates Passive Income, not Active Income (such as from a job or traditional business). Passive income will give you a "rechargeable bank account" that will grow or replenish month after month. You will be hiring a competent Property Manager to handle the day to day operation of your rental property. I will be reinforcing this concept again later, but understand that I am not training you to be a "landlord." I am training you to be a real estate investor. You will own the hamburger stand - not sit there flipping burgers… Hold that thought for now.

A Team Sport

There is no aspect of rental real estate you will have to be the final expert on. You will be surrounding yourself with experts.

Your job will be to gather and assess their knowledge and make decisions on where and when to invest based on your conclusions that are right for you as an investor based on their knowledge.

For example:

Your Realtor - will help you find the property.

Your Mortgage Broker - will tell you how to afford the property.

Your Property Manager - will help you assess the rentability of the property, find you a tenant, and manage the property day-by-day.

Your Property Inspector - will tell you anything wrong with the property before you buy it.

Your Insurance Agent - will get you the coverage you need as an investor

Your CPA - will help you operate the property like a business and pay the least amount of tax possible.

While other investors try to become the smartest person in the room to find answers for themselves, you will build a team who can tell you the answers right now. In this sense, you need the skill of finding and building relationships with experts far more than you need the skill of becoming one yourself.

Your job will simply be to lead the team toward the goals you have set forth - and that is why you need to be a knowledgeable investor.

All of these points lead me to the purpose of it all. With passive cash flow, leverage, simplicity, and a team…Rental real estate produces its ultimate fruit for you: *Freedom.*

Chapter 2:

The Power of Just One Rental

It can be easy to think that Rental Real Estate is an interesting hobby or side adventure that would be "nice" to have along with your 401(k) - but I would encourage you as you begin your journey toward your first rental property to really take seriously the impact that just one rental property can have on your financial future.

If you search online for the words "retirement crisis" you will find an endless stream of new articles of how most Americans are simply not saving enough for retirement - and some aren't saving at all. The cliché of the elderly Wal-Mart greeter is not fiction - it's real. Adding to this is the skyrocketing longevity of the human race! Back when Social Security was established, the average life expectancy was 60. You worked, had a few "golden years" and then died. Today, it is no big deal to meet someone in their 80's, and we will eventually all personally know at least someone in their 90's or even over 100 – that may even be us!

Why rental real estate is so powerful in helping this retirement crisis is because of the leverage and high returns that it makes possible relative to its highly controllable risk. As discussed more later in this book - you can literally calculate the returns you can expect from a rental property before you even purchase it - and frankly it's no big deal to find rental properties with a total annual Return-on-Investment (ROI) in the 12-15% range. Some of these rentals will look like extremely boring, simple houses you wouldn't think twice about if you were driving by – such as our rental on the cover of this book!

Contrast this with mainstream investing's notion that what you should be doing is putting all of your money in mutual funds that *may* produce you 10-12% per year over the *long term* (meaning not every year - and sometimes not every decade!) – but only if you are *"really aggressive"*. In fact, let's compare and contrast Rental Real Estate vs. Mutual Funds really quick…

Mutual Funds	Rental Real Estate
Need all the money yourself.	Bank will give you most of the money.
Returns to expect based on "past performance."	Returns to expect based on current reality.
No control.	High control.
Returns based on "the market."	Returns based on your choices as an investor.
Complex - Needs an "expert advisor."	Simple and Intuitive once skilled at the basics.
"Diversify" for safety.	Analyze for safety.
Intangible, Paper/ Electronic Asset	Tangible, Physical Asset
Retire when you are old.	Retire ASAP!

The list could go on and on…maybe one day I'll grab a bottle of wine and/or a pot of coffee and see how long of a list I can make. For now, let's proceed…

The Traditional 5% Return

A traditional financial adviser is going to suggest that during your "working years" that you invest in growth stocks or other such more aggressive mutual funds so that your nest egg can grow as big as possible before you retire. They will tell you that such "aggressive investments" *should* produce about a 10-12% average return *over the long-term,* meaning over *decades* (any one year – or one decade - could be a disaster). They will go on to say that this estimate is based on *past performance* and is not guaranteed.

But - once you are at "retirement age" (what a concept - like somehow, it's an age - yuck) the traditional advisor's advice is going to be to be conservative with your investment portfolio. This means you shouldn't expect to withdraw any more than 5% a year to live on - some advisors even say 4%. But let's run with 5%...

Let's say you had $25,000 saved up and you wanted to use it to create some supplemental retirement income. So what kind of income can you make assuming a 5% return on your "nest egg?"

At 5% a year, your $25,000 investment would produce $1,250 of interest income a year, or $104 per month. Now, since you are withdrawing that $104 per month, your $25,000 will always stay $25,000 because of course you aren't re-investing the income back into savings anymore (because you need the income to live on now) - so nothing is growing or compounding. After thirty years of retirement earning $104 a month you will have withdrawn $37,440 - and will still have the $25,000 you started with. So, in total, your $25,000 will have become an $62,440 impact in your life. Ok, cool.

The Rental Real Estate Alternative

On the other hand - let's say you took that $25,000 and purchased a $100,000 rental house by putting 20% down, plus closing costs, and borrowing 80% from the bank. You rent out the house for $1,000 a month, and after all monthly expenses you are able to receive $204 in monthly cash flow. After 30 years of retirement earning $204 a month you will have received a total of $73,440.

Also, after 30 years of making mortgage payments (with the rent your tenant has paid you), your tenant - not you, will have paid off your $80,000 mortgage. So, you will have withdrawn $73,440 and be sitting on a paid off house worth $100,000. That is if you never raised the rent and home prices hadn't changed in 30 years...cough - cough - (oh, excuse me - sorry - something in my throat).

So...

Plan A: Your $25,000 produces $104 a month and after 30 years it has all added up to a $62,440 impact on your retirement, or...

Plan B: Your $25,000 produces $204 a month – almost double of Plan A, and after 30 years it all adds up to a $173,400 impact on your retirement.

Hmm.... I would say Plan B, using rental real estate, is a bit of a no-brainer - but I can play the theme music to *Jeopardy* if you need time to think...

So, Brian, if it's this simple, why doesn't everybody invest in rental real estate instead? I'll tell you why exactly. Because mutual funds take zero education, zero involvement, and you can buy them $100 at a time automatically from your paycheck in a 401(k). "Everyone" is investing in mutual funds and options for doing so are simply handed to you by your employer. You can walk into any bank branch and the people over on the left sitting at the desks can sell you mutual funds.

On the other hand, rental real estate investing takes reading this book, taking responsibility, saving up, doing something that nobody you know may be doing, and taking action. That is just simply more than what most people are willing to go through. Looking further than that simple truth for an answer will send you into a fruitless eternal desert of mysterious wondering. But don't worry - you are reading this book - you have found the treasure map - so let us proceed.

P.S. - Personal Side Note...

By the way - confession time - I spent over 10 years of my life with my Securities License with FINRA (The Financial Industry Regulatory Authority). I was advising clients on their IRA's, 401(k)'s and Annuities. I was selling mutual funds from household-name companies and I was *forbidden* to advise my clients on anything that wasn't a "compliant investment product," which basically meant anything that wasn't on the mutual fund menu.

However, I never failed to mention rental real estate in passing to every client as something they may want to investigate on their own - because deep down I knew it was so much more powerful in helping them reach their financial goals. However, rental real estate would take a lot more hands-on work on their part because I couldn't magically help someone invest in real estate by filling out a form the way I could with a mutual fund.

Deep down, however, I knew the money I was helping them invest would hardly make a game-changing difference in their lives – it was just better than nothing. I knew that if they saved up and put that money to work in real estate instead that it could make a real difference. All I could do is encourage them to keep learning while they saved up money so that perhaps one day their knowledge and saved up capital could combine into an opportunity for them. This was largely wishful thinking on my part to make myself feel better.

This conflict within me culminated in the fact that I voluntarily terminated my Securities License a few years ago. Think of an attorney voluntarily terminating their license with the State Bar and you can imagine the emotional turmoil I went through. But, it's done, and I am free. And I am so happy to be preaching the gospel of Real Estate - Hallelujah!!!

(here's where you say "Amen!" lol).

PART 2

YOUR INVESTOR MINDSET

Chapter 3:

Becoming an Investor, not a Landlord

Before we continue your journey toward your first rental property (which you have already started if just by picking up this book), we need to re-classify some ideas you may have seen in the world around you regarding being a "landlord." That is because most of what you have likely seen, heard, and experienced regarding rental real estate was from complete amateur "landlords" that don't know what they are doing - and as a professional investor you are not to take their version of reality as true for you in any way - because as you will soon come to realize - their woes are almost completely self-inflicted.

You see, unless you are renting an apartment in a huge complex owned by a major corporation, most "landlords" you are likely to encounter are not only amateurs, they likely became a landlord by *accident.* Maybe they had a house they were trying to sell and it didn't sell in time and so they just decided to "rent it out." Maybe they inherited a house and they and their siblings can't decide what to do with mom's house, so they just "rent it out." Maybe they bought the house across the street when there was a good deal on it and they figured "heck - I'll just… (wait for it)…rent it out!" Lol

These accidental/amateur landlords ("AA Landlords?" Hmmm) are the people that whine at you about the "Terrible T's" of toilets and tenants. They make land-lording sound terrible. They have, or know someone that has, some horror story about land-lording that is powerful enough as a singular incident to deter anyone from ever owning a rental property.

Um, yea. That's not going to be you - and you are not to listen to these people that can needlessly crush your dreams if you take them seriously.

Because I am not training you to be a *landlord.*
I'm training you to be a *real estate investor.*

39

Pause and re-read the two previous lines slowly, and out loud if needed.

What do I mean by this? Well, here's the sad reality: Every time my wife and I look at a rental property for sale, we always try to ask why the seller is selling. The answer is almost always: "Because the seller wants to retire." What? My wife and I are trying to *buy* their rental property so we can retire! They want to *sell* it so they can retire? We run into this over, and over, and over. What gives?

Here's the deal - for them, they are the *landlord*, and they manage, and mismanage, and tinker, and futz with the property like a job, as if it is a hardware store or a sandwich shop. *They* mow the lawn, *they* get the calls to fix the toilet, *they* drive by the property because it's on their way home from their other job - and while they are driving by, the fact that the mail box is just a bit off center catches their eye - and now it's bothering *them* (but nobody else), so now that's their Saturday project. And at this point they have become best friends with their tenants and so they never feel right about raising the rent, and so after years and years go by they're getting totally screwed by the cheap rent.

With low rental income the amateur landlord becomes resentful when inevitable repairs are eventually required for any property, so they put off these repairs, which often leads to much more expensive repairs being needed later. Their ownership of this property is literally a part-time job they have to show up and work in - and selling it to us is a huge relief so they can "retire."

With so much deferred maintenance, the amateur landlord puts the property up for sale as a "fixer" at a price tens-of-thousands less than the property would be worth if it had been well kept. So, by being cheap on management and repairs, they will lose countless thousands in lost rent along the years, and a huge loss of sale value in the end. Meanwhile, the tenant has lived in a decaying home they have no incentive to fix themselves, or demand that the landlord perform repairs, lest dong so triggers a rent increase. I call this arrangement *Mutually-Assured Destruction*, and it is all too common.

Such is the plight of the amateur/accidental landlord. What hell. On the other hand, my wife and I have chosen to adopt the mentality and follow in the footsteps of a Professional Real Estate Investor, distinguished from amateur landlords by the fact that she and I run our rentals like a business and have an expert investment team (which this book will teach you to have as well).

As the professional investor you are training to be in this book you are going to be highly intentional with your rental acquisitions. You are going to analyze *up front* why a particular property is worth purchasing with rental, purchase, and financing data provided by your team. You are going to know the financial return your property will likely produce and decide on paper if a particular property is worth investing in long before you purchase one in real life.

Your team is going to tell you every possible flaw with the physical property before purchasing it as well as future repairs to look out for. You are going to research what the housing and economic trends are in the area the property is in, and your team is going to help you look at the property through the perspective of your future tenant and prepare the property with what will be important to them - not you.

Your team is going to perform a professional pre-screening of the financial viability and criminal background of every tenant they find for you. You are going to incentivize great tenants to stay for years and years while never letting your rents fall dramatically behind the going rate, or letting your property decay into disrepair. You are going to run a professional, real estate investing business - supported by a team of professionals - even if your entire business is starting with just one property you are renting to just one person. Build the team, habits, and systems now as you begin, and you will never have to look back.

We don't make a move without our team - we don't buy a property without our team - we know exactly what the numbers are on everything before we make a decision because of our team - I've never met or even spoken to our great tenants because of our team, and I've never personally gone to the hardware store and spent a Saturday making a repair on a property because of our team. And I'm free this evening to write this book and set our sights on doing more and more bigger deals - because of our team. Just like sitting in a restaurant, we are in charge of choosing what appears on our plate by running our team toward our investing goals, but we don't have to cook a thing.

Yikes! Isn't a team expensive? Not at all - in fact, they are going to give you a tremendous amount of guidance for free - and only get paid for the specific work they do, which is work that makes you money.

PART 3

RENTAL PROPERTY IS A TEAM SPORT

Chapter 4:

Meet Your Team

If you need to be the smartest person the room - you are going to have a very hard time building a rental real estate business. If you cut your own hair and fill your own dental cavities, you are going to have a very hard time building a rental real estate business. However, if you can have a vision, and then hire professionals to make it a reality, you are going to love the rental real estate business.

I'd like you to introduce you to your team. In a short while I'll tell you how to build one (or borrow one) of your own. Now, keep in mind, these are not your employees. They are professionals in their specialized field that you have built first-name basis relationships with. Much of your team has never met anyone else on your team. We, as the investors, are the center of our teams.

Now, before you get overwhelmed, keep in mind that many of these team members are only used once in a while (and a lot of them you will very easily find through referrals, as you will see). Once your new rental property is up and running smoothly (referred to as "stabilized"), you will likely mainly only communicate with your property manager. And...you'll never have to build a team again in that same market area.

For now, read and relax as you see all of the many things that your team will be doing for you. The following is a list of the members of your team.

Investor-Minded Real Estate Agent

The very first, anchor-member of your team is an investor--minded real estate agent. I say "investor-minded" because it is critical that the real estate agent (aka: Realtor, Real Estate Broker) that you use can look at properties as rental investment, not just as retail family homes for someone to purchase and live in themselves.

Yes, you want to know big things about a property and a neighborhood such as crime rates, but you are less concerned with the exact color of the kitchen countertops or other issues that perhaps would matter more to you if you were a retail-buyer looking to purchase and live in the home. Your real estate agent is going to be a great source of things you need to know like neighborhood desirability, and overall trends of where a city's growth and progress is heading. But don't get lost in the color of the drapes, and if your agent is - find a different one!

Property Manager

Tied in importance, or perhaps in the long term of even of more importance than a real estate agent, is a property manager. You want a relationship with a property manager *before* you purchase a rental property. Think of a property manager as your salesperson. Wouldn't you want to know that the "product" you are about to produce (your rental property) is something that the salesperson can "sell?"

You do this by bringing in a property manager early on in your property hunt. Get their approval that the property you are considering is in an area, and is of a size and condition that will easily rent - and them have them tell you what market rent is in that area. You will never have to guess about the potential rental income of a property because of our property manager. You may even get a tip about where rentals are in demand, so you can hunt in that area for a property (only if that property also meets your personal investment criteria as we will discuss).

Investor- Minded Mortgage Broker

Rounding out the top-three of indispensable, key team members is your investment-minded mortgage broker. You want a mortgage broker that really understands rental properties, and can guide you in what to expect in terms of costs, and process in purchasing a property. We never guess about what down payment we would need, what an interest rate is, what closing costs are, etc. because we simply call our mortgage broker and brainstorm my ideas. We tell our mortgage broker our dreams and then he tells us the actual reality of what that would take to accomplish them - and usually he has amazing ideas for getting them done we didn't even consider. And why would we have? He's the expert!

Property Inspector

You will never purchase a property without paying for your own, professional property inspection. We've literally been in Escrow about to close on a property when a home inspector stopped me cold and saved us (apparently termites had eaten the entire foundation of what was otherwise a lovely looking, quaint triplex). We are not qualified to know what is serious in terms of property repairs, and what is simply a cosmetic issue we can fix later. But, a qualified home inspector is qualified, and you always, always want one on your side. Your Inspection Report created by your inspector is also a negotiating tool your real estate agent can use to further negotiate concessions from the seller, even after an initial purchase price has been agreed upon. In short, a great property inspector never costs you money - they save you money…and potential disaster.

General Handyman

You may have your own handyman, or your property manager may know one (or have one on staff), but however you get one, they are indispensable. A general handyman can do all of the small, knicky-knack repairs that would be costly to have a specialized technician come do one-by-one. Since you have an ongoing relationship with your handyman, you will likely get the best prices on his repairs, and you can ultimately trust him to be a mini-inspector of sorts, letting you know up front if a repair a property needs is something in his capabilities before you purchase the property. If not, you will need specialized technicians, which leads us to our next team members.

Specialized Technicians

A general handyman is a lifesaver, but when it comes to specialized technicians, like Electricians, Plumbers, Pest Control, Radon Gas Remediation, Heating/AC specialists, and Rooter technicians, you are going to have to call in a specialized pro. It is crucial to have relationships so that they will move quickly and charge you fairly when the time comes. Your real estate agent should have referrals to these people to begin with - but then you want to treat them right and develop your own relationship and rapport with them.

Title / Escrow Officer

A title and escrow officer should be someone that your real estate agent or mortgage broker already has a great relationship with, but then you want to build your own relationship with them and consider them their own member of your team. Any time you need to understand property taxes, property title, or you need to arrange for one of your technicians to be paid directly from escrow (another favorite trick we can talk about later), you are going to want to be able to reach out to your title/escrow team member for a quick answer.

Investor-Savvy Attorney

When you are starting out on your real estate investing journey, you will want to talk to a competent attorney that specializes in real estate investors. This attorney can talk to you about the possible benefits of setting up a formal company to hold and operate your property, such as an LLC. Once you are on track legally, you will likely not need to consult your attorney very often, but having that relationship pre-built in case you need them in the future can be invaluable. Otherwise, most of the contracts such as lease agreements, etc. involved in the day-to-day operation of your rental business will be provided by your property manager.

Investor-Savvy CPA (Certified Public Accountant)

This is one of my favorite team members. The tax advantages to rental real estate investing are mind-blowing. I've mentioned some of the tax advantages previously, but suffice it to say, you need a CPA that specializes in real estate investors. Like a property inspector, a CPA does not cost you money, they make you money.

You are in a real business now, and you have officially out-grown Turbo-Tax, Uncle Bob, your buddy's "tax-prep guy," or H&R Block on the corner. Those outlets are for employees with a W-2 job going on and that's it. You are an investor/business-owner and you don't even know what you don't know so you don't know how to even ask. There are advanced tax strategies only available to business owners and real estate investors that will blow your mind – and laws are changing all the time.

But, if you don't know how to take advantage of these laws the IRS does not exactly mind. They make a lot of money on amateur landlords that don't know any better. Avoid missing out and get a great CPA on your side. It is also a helpful bonus if your CPA has some basic relationship with your attorney if that is possible, so they are on the same page about what you have going on (one can usually refer you to the other if not).

Investor-Savvy Insurance Broker

As an investor, you have different insurance needs than does a typical homeowner. Yes, you want to protect the structure of your building in case of fire or other damage. But, you also need to be protected from other liabilities such as injuries that can occur on your property, and loss of income while your property is repaired after a catastrophe, etc. What you do not need, however, are any "homeowner" items covered like the personal property, TV's, etc. inside the building that belongs to your tenant (those items are exactly what "Renter's Insurance" is for!).

It's a whole new mindset as an investor, and a great investor-savvy insurance broker can get you all the right coverage, without paying for things you don't need, all at a great price. Your insurance broker can also help you think through whether your property is in a Flood Plane (which is an official designation for certain areas of the country) or has any other special considerations you should know about up-front so you can put the cost of the proper insurance coverage in your analysis prior to purchasing the property. Having a precise number for insurance cost to put in an analysis can make or break the profitability of a deal, so don't underestimate the power of this, often under-celebrated, team member.

Now, all of these team players may seem like a lot - but don't be overwhelmed. I'm going to teach you how to build (or borrow) a team like this - and with email, phone, credit cards, and a local realtor to physically un-lock a property - you can do just about anything long distance these days without physically being there even if you happen to live or work far away from where you will be investing.

A Team in Action

Like conducting a great orchestra, a team in concert with itself can make beautiful music. Your "conductor's baton" in this case, however, are just phone calls and emails...

I thought you would enjoy an example of exactly how a team can work together - all with your simple coordination. So, here's a real-life example that happened when we were purchasing a rental property:

My wife and I had recently visited Indiana where we found the rental property, but then once we were in escrow we came back to California to resume our lives. So, all of this happened by email and phone calls on lunch breaks while I worked full time in California (how cool is that!). All of this is possible because of a team - and a team built on trust and relationships (which I will show you how to build). Here goes...

Once you are under-contract for the purchase of a property, you now "open escrow," and get a "due diligence" period of time during which you can conduct any home inspections, etc. you may wish to do to make sure the property is in the condition you think it is in. So, our real estate agent arranged for our property inspector to access this property to do a full inspection.

The inspector noticed that it needed some electrical work to be safe. My property inspector emailed us a full inspection report highlighting the work that needed to be done, complete with photographs, and we talked about it over the phone.

We then emailed this inspection report to our electrician. The report was so thorough and had such great pictures that our electrician didn't even need to visit the property to write up an estimate for the repairs! Our electrician simply emailed me a detailed invoice of what it would cost to do the work. I emailed that invoice to my real estate agent, who then used it to negotiate us a credit from the seller for the cost to do that work. The seller agreed, and my real estate agent arranged for the property to be opened for the electrician to do the work, and I emailed his invoice straight to the title/escrow team member so they could mail a check to the electrician at the close of escrow. Boom! I had electrical repairs done at a property in Indiana while I sat at my desk in California. How cool is that!

While my wife and I are investing long-distance – please know that the same concept fully applies if you happen to end up investing near where you live. You want a team of experts to communicate with each other and get the task at hand handled professionally. You don't want to screw it up by being the "expert" – you simply stand in the middle and conduct the orchestra of actual experts you have built. Remember - the only thing you have to be an expert in is what your investment goals are, and how to build the relationships to make them a reality.

Chapter 5:

Property Management

While a Property Manager was listed prominently in the last chapter as a critical member of your team, I have seen new investors experience a great deal of confusion, and even resistance, over the topic of property management.

Because I believe so strongly in the importance of professional property management, *even if you live local to your property,* I wanted to dedicate an entire chapter here so that you can at least really understand everything you need to consider in choosing whether or not to hire a manager.

If you decide to become your own property manager, you are taking full responsibility for everything a manager does, and a great property manager does far more than simply find a tenant for you. A great property manager will:

Provide Accurate Data for Investment Analysis

- Give you the rental-rate data you need to analyze what will be a great rental property before you even buy it *and* the rentability (demand) for the property you are considering given its physical nature, condition, and location.

Protect You from Your Tenants

- Un-emotionally screen and place fantastic tenants – using factors that go far beyond what a potential tenant's credit score may say (good or bad), including job stability, rent-to-income ratio, responsiveness and personality exhibited during the application process, and feedback from previous landlords, just to name a few.

- Be an un-emotional facilitator of both reasonable repairs or needs of the tenant *and* annual rental increases as the years (and decades) go by.

53

- Be an advisor on tenant retention, and coordinate gifts or other incentives to keep tenants happy.

Protect Your Time

- Collect rent and deal with issues on your behalf, 24 hours a day, 365 days a year, including holidays and weekends, resolving most minor issues before you even become alerted to their existence.

Protect Your Property

- Be "eyes and ears" for you on the condition of your property – both outside, and also inside as they, or their handyman, visit the property seasonally to replace A/C filters, etc.

- Be a golden source of handymen, and other repair experts at preferred prices as needs arise.

Keep Your Books Organized

- Be an expert book-keeper keeping track of all of your profit and expenses, creating monthly and annual statements for you to simply hand to your CPA at tax time.

Protect You Legally

- Manage your property in full-awareness of all legal compliance issues, such as possible local rent-control laws, and for the proper procedural treatment of a tenant in good times and bad (and have an attorney on speed-dial on your behalf for any highly unlikely major issues that may arise beyond their expertise, such as going to court for an eviction, etc.).

Partner in Future Strategic Planning

- A manager is connected with lots of other investors they manage property for, and as such, they essentially are the center of an informal investor network. Every other investor's property serves as a test-case for you, giving your manager a collective source of ideas to maximize the rentability and profit potential of your property, as well as referrals to other team members and vendors for you.

- Inside track for other property they manage that may come up for sale before anyone else even knows.

If you really digest everything a great property manager will do - I would say they are under-paid. Most work on commission – only taking 10% or so of the gross rent of the tenant they have found for you each month. Some may also charge an additional fee for actually placing the tenant in the first place – but this is all just subtracted from the rent.

In other words, your property manager doesn't get paid a dime until they help you make a dollar. You will never write a check to a manager, except perhaps in the very beginning of the relationship to put in a reserve account so they can act upon repair requests quickly on your behalf. In the end, a great property manager will not cost you money – they will make you money.

The Biggest Benefit of all: Protecting You from Yourself

While a great property manager can help avoid and solve problems, it's when things go perfectly well that a manager can really protect you from the most profit-killing threat of all: *yourself.* Specifically, a professional manager will protect you from lost revenue and equity over the years inflicted by gushy self-management that you will absolutely be tempted to slip into on your own. Here's what I mean:

Let's say you forego hiring a manager and instead find a tenant on your own, and they actually turn out to be great tenants. They pay their rent on-time and never call you for repairs. As the months go by, you and your tenant are getting along wonderfully and they are becoming your new "buddy." Great, right?

So now a year comes and goes and your tenant is happy to stay and keep paying rent indefinitely into the future. At this point are you really going to serve your new buddy with a rental increase for the new year to keep up with market rent? Hello no!

What's going to happen is that since they pay on time and have never bothered you for a repair request, you are going to figure why "rock the boat." Instead, you will leave the rent the same for next year and by doing so you will have trained them *not* to report property issues to you. This silent pact of "You don't complain about repairs and I won't raise the rent" sets up an expectation for next year, and the year after that, to work out the same. I refer to this pattern as ***Mutually-Assured Destruction.*** Here's how it works:

Because you never raised the rent each year to market levels (as allowed by local law), you missed out on $20 per month more last year, and $35 more a month this year, and so on. Fast-forward 10 years and that is thousands of dollars. Oh, and those minor repairs you trained them *not* to call you about? Yea, well, that $100 minor bathroom leak is now a $10,000 mold problem, and that $15 AC/Furnace filter is now a $7,000 unit that burned out too soon with improper maintenance.

So, you missed out on increased rent along the way, and years later you're sitting as the proud owner of a run-down property, and now you want to sell it so you can "retire" from the land-lording business. Yes, you saved a management fee – and you will never know what that cost you. And the thing is, it all happens so slowly you don't even realize it's happening.

Can't my Realtor just Find a Tenant for me, then I can Manage the property myself from there?

You may find a real estate agent who personally *is* a property manager. If this is the case, don't get too excited too soon. Make sure this agent really has a team in place to be an effective full-time property manager and they aren't just saying they are willing to "help you find a tenant" or something incomplete like that, which many Realtor's will be more than happy to try to do.

I deeply respect the value of what a great Realtor does when they are doing what they do best – which is help you navigate and negotiate a great property acquisition. A great Realtor is a source of invaluable referrals to other members of your team, and will be a key player in your success as an investor. Likewise, a full-blown property manager does what they do best – which is act on your behalf in *all* aspects of your rental business. There is just no way a real estate agent can "also" be a property manager all by themselves unless they have a legitimate property-management company and a support team of their own.

Like buying a puppy, getting a tenant is only the beginning of the journey, and everything is great on Christmas Morning when everyone is playing with this new puppy. But what about when it's time for some tough work of training the puppy and taking it to the vet? What about when the tenant gets laid off or has an issue with the neighbor? What about when the state you live in updates it's laws about what a "comfort animal" is so now your pet deposit is illegal - or changes what notice you need to give a tenant before you enter the property?

Landlord-Tenant Law has multiple layers to it. There are State Laws that must be followed, then there can be City Ordinances that over-lay State Law, and, if you have a Home Owner's Association connected with your property they will have their own Bylaws concerning renting your property.

In my home state a law just recently quietly passed placing nearly all property in the entire state under rent-control. Is your property an exception? Are you staying on top of that all day, day after day? Is your Realtor? Can you call them when you have a problem and they will jump in and fix it, or did they get paid in the beginning by finding you a tenant/buying you a puppy and they are long gone by now? Or, are you going to have a landlord-tenant law attorney on retainer so you can call them at a moment's notice for help?

Final Thoughts:

With all of the changing laws, potential lawsuits, property decay and lost rent waiting for you as a property owner if you handle a tenant inappropriately, I am more likely to drill my own teeth than I am to manage my own property. I say this even though *I am* a licensed Realtor and have the investing experience I do. I just have my own job to do as the professional investor at the head of our investment team, which is building relationships and finding our next deal. These are tasks only you as the investor can do.

Yes, my Aunt Laura managed her own property. She was retired, she had all day to deal with anything that came up, legally it was a simpler time, and she was no longer expanding her portfolio and looking for new deals. If that describes you, then go for it - I am not going to say *never* manage your own property, but I am going to say be prepared, and understand that doing so will take your time and mental energy away from what only you as an investor can do – which is to find your next deal.

Management is simply its own profession, and requires a full-time commitment to do properly. By managing your own property, you instead will have jumped in the kitchen of your own restaurant and started flipping burgers – taking the spatula out of the hand of a professional chef that is better than you are at flipping burgers, food safety laws, etc., and would have worked for you for a reasonable wage.

To maximize the value you will get out of your property manager stay engaged with them, reach out and let them know you appreciate them, ask pro-active questions, and make it clear you value their opinion. Many managers may not wish to "bother" you unless there is an issue to deal with – make it clear you are a forward-thinking investor and make sure to touch base with your manager perhaps every season or two – even if there aren't any pressing issues to discuss. The result will be turning your property manager into a true business partner and friend.

Chapter 6:

How to Build a Team

Pick a Location

Before you begin to build a team – you must first decide exactly where you are going to be investing. You want your team to be local to that area. So, you may wish to finish the other chapters of this book that will teach how to select an area, and then circle-back to this chapter then. I'm including how to build a team now, however, because in case the last chapters intimidated you, I want to reassure you that building a team really isn't that big of a deal.

Finding Your Realtor

As you now know, you are in the center of your team, but then a major cornerstone of the team is a real estate agent. So now we need to find one that is:

1) A responsive, kind, professional person.
2) Understands investors, not just "retail homebuyers."
3) Enjoys the fact that you are new to investing (especially if you are doing so long-distance).

Here's how to find and audition a real estate agent to see if you click with them on all of these levels:

Now, I know I haven't taught you yet how to identify a good rental property yet, but once you have identified a price range and general geographic area for your property search (using the methods yet to be discussed later in this book), I would identify 3 potential properties of general interest, and reach out to the 3 real estate agents representing those homes.

As you prefer - make a call or send an email to all 3 of the agents from each 3 of the properties you selected. Tell them "My name is such and such, and I'm calling from (whatever city you live in) -

I'm reaching out to you because I saw your listing of 123 Main St., and I'm looking for possible rental property like this."

Now, if you call them and speak with them live - then great. If not, *I almost prefer getting their voice mail or sending them an email because that is a great test of how fast they get back to you.* Any Realtor worth a darn getting a potential new client calling them out of the blue will absolutely get back to you immediately (unless they are in the hospital having major surgery – then it might take 24 hours lol). New leads like you are what they live for (did I mention I'm also a Realtor? lol) - and here you are dropping yourself in their lap. They need to make getting back to you a priority.

You might email with these real estate agents to make an initial contact, but ultimately you want to speak to your potential real estate agent as soon as possible live on the phone. Only speaking with someone live can you get a real sense of their personality. So, if they've been responsive in getting back to you, and when you speak with them they've been personable and professional, then they meet requirement #1. The next step is to see if they have the eye for working with investors.

In your conversation with them, make it clear that you are looking for rentals and that you are an investor - and that you live where you do. Just hit them with all of these facts all at once. This will automatically elicit some sort of reply. Here are some possible responses:

If they say: "I've heard of people investing here, how did you hear about our city?" or, "Well, I work with all types of clients and I'd love to help you if I can…"

*Then you should be thinking: **"PASS!"***

But, if they say something much closer to: "I work with a lot of investors, most of my investors are out of state, some are local, and I own and manage several rental properties of my own"

*Then you should be thinking: **"JACKPOT!"***

You might think I'm making things a little too black-and-white here, but it really goes down pretty much exactly like this. Real estate agents are either immediately going to know exactly what you're talking about as an investor, or investing is a foreign language they don't speak and can't fake.

Now, you might get a real estate agent that says they have a partner in the office that handles investors, etc. - then that's ok - get a referral to them and start the same process of screening them. You can also simply call the real estate office the listing agent you found is from and ask for the branch manager. Then ask the manager who they would say is the best agent for an investor like you. Believe me – you are not bothering these agents or managers! This is what they live for, and someone calling out of the blue who might want to buy real estate is what they dream about at night.

You will know you are dealing with a real estate agent you really click with if when you get off the phone with them, all of the following is happening:

1) You genuinely enjoyed speaking with them - they were friendly, maybe you shared a laugh, but they also really seemed confident in what they were saying. Remember that this is someone you are eventually going to meet, spend a day with, eat with, drive many miles with, and speak with endlessly on the phone. You have to simply like them for this journey to work! Don't settle for a "meh" connection with someone. This is not your butcher - this is a business partner (though I actually love my butcher too - darn - bad example - but you know what I mean!).

2) They shared insights into the rental market - areas to invest in - and even aspect of properties that make good rentals you wouldn't have thought of (maybe having central gas heat vs. electric heat, or whatever is desired in that area) or perhaps tax rates associated with different parts of town, etc. - whatever it is, just some tidbit of local knowledge from their own experience that gives you confidence that they've been around the block.

3)   You hang up with them having plans for them to email listings of properties for sale to you to start looking through to see as examples of potential rental properties - and plans to speak again after you have taken a look.

If those three things happen - you are off to a great start.

The Power of Coffee

So, your new possible real estate agent (we are still auditioning them) emails you a list of potential rental properties. The next thing to do is to get your Realtor on the phone and go through the list of properties they have sent you - while you can both be in front of a computer.

Go one by one through the properties and ask the agent whey they thought it was a good candidate. In going through the list, you will hear how they think when choosing a property - you will hear their input regarding the area each property is in, and you will get a sense of whether you like the way they think. Also, you can tell in the conversation if the agent has the patience to be a bit of a teacher, explaining why certain things are the way they are in their city, and what to look for on each property because of those local needs, etc.

If you get off the phone with the sense that both A) There are really some great rentals in this city, and B) this Realtor is definitely the person to guide you through them, then here's what you do next...

Email your new real estate agent with a thank you email, and separately email them a $10 Starbucks gift card. (You can go to www.Starbucks.com and send one straight from there to their email). This thanks the agent for their time that they have been investing in you for free and you will instantly stand apart by miles from all of the other people happy to waste their time. Whether you buy a property with this agent soon or not, you will instantly be in their "this person appreciates me" list - and you will be amazed how far this gets you.

You will likely start seeing a pattern in the list of properties you are discussing with your new agent, and soon you will be on the hunt (on your computer, or perhaps even in person) for properties in certain areas you have identified. Soon you will be noticing properties on your own, sending a link to them to your agent, and asking "what do you think of this one?" – or "what do you think of this area?" The back-and-forth will be productive as you refine your eye for a good rental in that city.

At this point - whether you use them exclusively as your only agent or not, I would say it's fair to count them as "your" real estate agent! Your team is starting to take shape! And good news - your real estate agent is probably able to refer you to most of the rest of your team! Let's take a look...

Finding Your Property Manager

A property manager will be the very next key part of your team that you will need prior to purchasing any property at all. Ask your new real estate agent for a referral to a property manager. If they work with investors the chances are they will instantly have a property manager they can refer you to that they know very well.

If for whatever reason your real estate agent doesn't know a great property manager (or even perhaps a larger management company with a personal connection to someone there) – and it would be very surprising if they didn't - then your next job will be to source one. To do so I would start with Yelp reviews and put in a few calls following the same general process as you used to feel-out a good real estate agent. Tell them exactly what's going on - where you live (nearby / out-of-state, wherever you live), that you are working with a local real estate agent - and that you are starting small.

The same criteria will apply in feeling-out a property manager as it did when auditioning a real estate agent: are they knowledgeable, are they kind, are they patient with teaching you a bit as you go along - are they responsive? If you get the same good vibe from them that you get from your real estate agent -

then proceed with developing the relationship. Also - if you had a much better relationship with this new property manager than you did with your real estate agent – don't be afraid to work the system backwards and ask this property manager for a referral to a real estate they know and trust better.

Once you have a real estate agent and property manager in mind - loop them into contact with each other right away. Email the property manager the listings your real estate agent supplied you, and then have the same phone call with the manager about the property list as you had with your agent. Which ones do they like and why? You are quickly going to learn a ton about little things that matter to renters in your local market that don't necessarily mean anything to you where you live personally. You're going to hear things like "I like this one because it's close to a bus line" - or "There's a new hospital going in down the street from here, this is a good location," or of course, you will hear reasons why certain properties are not good. You may even hear tips for other parts of town to hunt in that fit your criteria.

Remember, at the end of the day, your property manager is your salesperson, and you and your real estate agent are the "product development team" for what your salesperson has to eventually sell. So, wouldn't it make sense to ask your salesperson what people are actually buying these days before going out and producing a product for them to sell? That's exactly what you are doing when you bring a property manager into your purchase decision at the beginning of the process. I would expect that by the time you actually own a property that your property manager and real estate agent will have been on the phone together, or even have been standing in the same property together, several times.

Finding Your Mortgage Broker

The next person to ask your real estate agent to refer you to is an investment – minded mortgage broker. Your real estate agent, property manager, and mortgage broker make up the primary trio of your team, and they will have the most direct interaction with each other, and play the largest role in your purchase. If your real estate agent doesn't know a great mortgage broker - which would be shocking - you will then instead source one through your property manager or even Yelp if you really had to.

If you are purchasing a single-family home (not a larger apartment building), just about any mortgage broker your real estate agent will refer you to would have expertise on that - but it will be very nice if you can find one with experience and passion for investors. If you are buying a duplex, triplex, or quadplex (also called a 2, 3, or 4 "unit" property) - technically these are all still classified as "Residential" real estate - so the same mortgage broker should be able to help you with either a single-family home, all the way up to a 4-plex. (Once you are purchasing an apartment complex with 5 or more units – that is considered "Commercial" real estate, and that is a completely different beast entirely, requiring you talk to a different mortgage broker).

Just as with a Realtor, finding a Mortgage Broker that really understands investors is going to be critical, because there are a lot of powerful elements in investment property that don't exist in owner-occupied transactions.

For example, it may be possible to count your expected rental income now in helping you qualify for the purchase of the property you don't even own yet! Again, this is the world of an experienced investor-minded mortgage broker and finding one is your next big win. Reach out to them right away - explain yourself and your goals - and let them teach you and guide you through what you are going to need to do.

Such a mortgage expert worthy of being on your team will likely not be the "mortgage guy" at your local bank branch, which is why I'm saying you need a real mortgage broker that can look at all of the lending programs available for investors like you instead of just being able to offer one bank's "brand" of product.

Our mortgage broker, Steve, poured hours and hours of education into us months before we purchased our first rental. A great mortgage broker wants to build this kind of relationship with you. He is now my first call for anything. Any time I have any questions about anything relating to mortgages I simply call our mortgage broker and not only does he have the answer to my question right away, he helps to creatively think through five new things I never would have thought to ask.

I would strongly encourage you to meet (even if it's only by phone) and start working with a mortgage broker as soon as possible. Even if you think you are months, or even over a year away from really making a move on purchasing a property, a mortgage broker can help you prepare. Your mortgage broker will likely ask you to fill out a loan application so they can pull your credit and really guide you on where you stand. If you have had a good connection with them up to that point – fill out that application! Your mortgage broker is on your team! Maybe your credit needs help, or based on your qualifications you need more down payment to get the property you want, etc. That's great stuff to know! Take advantage of this free, professional guidance.

Additional Team Referral Sources

If your Realtor and Yelp aren't leading you where you want to go with a great mortgage broker - the next place I would ask (and have asked) is at a Title/Escrow Company. A Title/Escrow Company is going to see all sorts of transactions all day long - single family, multi family, investors, etc. I would call out of the blue and ask a Title Officer there "Hey, who are the Mortgage Brokers you see closing a lot of deals for investors that really know what they are doing, and are really great to work with?" In other words, real estate in any town is a small world – and all real estate agents, mortgage brokers, title officers, etc. all work with lots of other real estate agents, mortgage brokers, title reps, etc.! Don't be afraid to ask around the circle for referrals!

Once you are armed with your core team members of a real estate agent, property manager, and mortgage broker, you are ready to get serious about narrowing down your initial general search, and actually identifying, analyzing, and purchasing a specific property. The rest of your team will be built as you go forward in this process, and will be fully built by the time your get the keys to your new property. For now, these first three key team members are who is going to help you find a property and get you the numbers you need to do property analysis with – and so they are all you need on your team for now to proceed with your property search.

PART 4

SELECTING A RENTAL PROPERTY

Chapter 7:

What the Goal of
Your First Rental Property Should Be

What is going to make the acquisition of your first rental property go much smoother than it otherwise would is if we start out with the right mindset. That starts by having the right goals and expectations for your first piece of rental real estate. I believe that you should have the same goals for your first experience investing in rental real estate as you would if you were to have your first experience driving a race car or skydiving. In short – don't die! Lol. Here's what I mean:

Your first time in a race car, you want to get the feel for the car and its limits. You want to see exactly what you can rely on from each member of your pit crew, and you need to learn practical things like how to heavy-duty seat belts click together. Most of all, expect to have a few spin-outs, but you don't want to crash straight into a wall.

Now, if along with all of this, you also happen to go fast – then that's great. Your first experience teaches you a ton of things that you'll never have to learn again so that next time you won't have to spend any energy worrying about the basics – and instead you can fully concentrate on going fast.

I think this exact same mentality will serve you well in approaching your first rental property. For your first rental, your goal should be to pick a market, build a team, learn how to analyze property, and emotionally feel what the process of acquiring a rental property is like. Don't worry about making a killing, worry about not crashing and losing money.

Have an educational adventure! Focus on learning how to be a disciplined investor that sticks to the rules on investing as you screen and select a property. Develop the habits of thinking in terms of reality, not hope – and factor in some failure into your analysis so that delays, unexpected expenses, and repairs don't spin you out emotionally.

With the right mentality, team, and analysis, there's no reason why your first rental property can't be profitable and successful right off the bat.

Before you know it, you'll own your first property, it will be working out great, and frankly you'll be a bit bored and itchy for the next one. Perfect! At that point you'll know a market, have a great team, and you'll be ready to roll either into more aggressive strategies, or to simply duplicate the great experience you just had with another property just like it.

Experienced rental real estate investor, Bill Manassero, wisely states that your education as an investor really begins *after* your first rental property. So, if that's true, let's not make it so scary up front that we don't get into the game! Today, Bill has decided to up-scale into large apartment buildings from the single-family homes he started with, and so his advice to you as a new investor may be different than mine in terms of where to begin your investing experience. But, I know Bill would agree with me that, like riding a bike, you can't learn what it's like to invest in rental property just by reading about it - you have to experience it in real life. When you do, so much intangible insight and wisdom gained in the process will be yours, forever.

Keep it Simple

Your first rental property should be bite-sized, both in terms of price and size (meaning "unit-count," which we will discuss in a minute). You want to be able to sleep at night knowing that you aren't in over your head, and that the worst-case-scenario of having to pay all of the expenses yourself for a while if you don't have a tenant really doesn't scare you. For example, the mortgage payment on your first rental was just a few hundred dollars, which is closer to a car payment than what one coming from California would think of a mortgage payment.

On the same note, your first rental property should probably be a property that is already in pretty good shape, and in an area that is fairly nice – even if that means you pay a little more for a nicer house in a nicer area and give up a little potential investment return percentage. There is so much that is going to be new and strange about investing – especially if you are doing so long-distance, it will be helpful if deep down on an emotional, gut-level that you can say to yourself "this is a nice property on a cute street, and I know people are going to love living here."

If the math is bite-sized, and emotionally it's a nice property, your blood pressure should stay reasonably low. So what if your first rental property only makes 8% a year instead of 18%. If the 8% property is one you can feel comfortable with enough to actually purchase – then you are in the game – and with the confidence and knowledge that will give you there's no telling the fortune you may be able to amass as you scale from there.

The great news is that in many ways your first rental will be the hardest. After your first rental is up and running, you have your team built, and you have a new sense of accomplishment and momentum - you can take all of that into your next deal, and your next. Your efforts and confidence will compound, and that's an exciting feeling.

Remember – I'm here to help you get into your first rental property – from zero to investor – from nothing to something. Are you bored after your first rental is stabilized and performing nicely? Then you're done something right! This should be boring! Horse Racing should be exciting. Roller coasters should be exciting. The best rental properties, like the best trips to the doctor, are the boring ones.

Chapter 8:

The 1% Rule

At this point, you have come far enough on your rental real estate quest to be considered an investing adolescent - and so, before things go further, you deserve to learn about the "birds and the bees" of spotting a potentially-great rental property. It's called "The 1% Rule."

The 1% Rule is how you are going to very quickly determine the potential viability of a rental property as a profitable investment. The 1% Rule states that if a property can rent each month for 1% of its purchase price - that it deserves closer analysis as a potential rental.

For example - if a property costs $100,000 to purchase - and it can be confidently rented for $1,000 a month (1% of its purchase price) - then it meets the 1% Rule and it is worth taking a closer look and doing a more thorough analysis.

The easiest way to quickly see this ratio of home prices vs. rental rates is on a website you may know of called Zillow.com. You can search for an area on a map - and then filter the results so that homes for sale - and homes for rent - appear at the same time.

Here is a screen shot of an example I found in just a few minutes searching around (in Indiana if you're curious)...

At the top left of the picture there is a home currently for sale for $155,000 - and then off to the bottom right is a home in the same neighborhood for rent for $1,500 - which is pretty much exactly the 1% Rule. Here's another example I found (this time in Texas)...

Now, does this mean these will make perfect rental-houses? No! But if you see multiple examples of the 1% Rule in a neighborhood, then it's probably an area worth doing some fishing in.

For some cities, the 1% Rule will be found in a higher price range than others. For other cities, the 1% won't be found at all. Your job as an investor is to find the sweet spot where the 1% Rule exists, in a neighborhood type you desire (as will be discussed soon), in a price range you can afford. Your team will do the rest - but this analysis and determination of your investing goals is your one and only job as an Investor.

Can you ever break the 1% Rule? Yes! Absolutely! This is just a quick-and-dirty initial check to see if a property, or an area, is close enough to be worth analyzing further. There are many very worthy rental-properties that won't conform to the 1% Rule exactly, but that offer other advantages that make you more comfortable as an investor or offer other benefits you like. You will know for yourself as you train your investor's "eye."

In the coming chapters you are going to learn how to think through the property type, size, price range, and city that feels like the best move for you as your first rental property. As you learn each piece new things will click in your mind – but don't get out ahead of yourself – wait until you've digested all of the chapters and then things will be clear....

Chapter 9:

What Size Property Should I Buy?

Rental properties come in different sizes – both physically, but more importantly in terms of unit count. Staying away from large apartment buildings for this discussion, your options for your first rental property likely include:

A Single-Family Home (1 Unit)

Or, a smaller Multi-Family Home, which may include:

A Duplex (Two Units)
A Triplex (Three Units)
A Fourplex or "Quad-Plex" (4 Units)

A single-family, 1-unit property is really its own animal – and then a 2 to 4-unit property is its own animal (there isn't really a big fundamental difference among the 2, 3, and 4-unit properties for our purposes here). So, you effectively have two choices in property size for your first rental property- either a single-family property, or a multi-unit property.

You may think that the question of how large of a property you should buy as your first rental property will be completely determined by what you can afford, but this isn't true. Believe it or not, it is usually possible to obtain a single-family home, vs. a duplex, etc. at about the same price (though perhaps in different parts of town). Regardless of price, you need to understand the differences between a single-family or multi-family rental property so you can make your own decision.

Again, I'm going to limit discussion here to the choice between a single-family home, and a small multi-unit such as a duplex, triplex, or quadplex (4-plex). Eventually you may wish to consider larger apartment buildings. But, for your first property, let's talk the difference between a single family, and a 2 to 4-unit property.

Single-Family vs. Multi-Family - Pro's & Cons

The advantages and disadvantages of single-family vs. multi-family properties are mirror-opposites of each other, meaning that an advantage to one is a disadvantage to the other. So, it is likely the easiest to explain this topic by simply giving you the advantages to each type of property:

The Advantages of Single-Family Homes:

One of the largest advantages to single family homes as your first rental property (let alone possibly your first long-distance rental property) is that emotionally and intellectually you already completely understand it. A single-family home, specifically a 3-bedroom single-family home, is the "fast ball down the middle," classic, vanilla ice-cream scoop of rental real estate.

You can literally find single family homes up and down every residential street in America. If you haven't lived in a single-family home, you know someone who has. There will be very little new to swallow emotionally or intellectually about owning this type of rental property. What you will have to learn of course is how to think through which one to purchase through an investor's eye - but in terms of the structure itself and why someone would want to live in it, you already have that level of understanding.

Aside from the emotional familiarity that a simple, single-family home will bring you, we can see some strategic advantages as well: A single-family home is simply more plentiful in the marketplace than multi-unit properties, so you will have the widest possible selection to choose from if you select to pursue the purchase of this type of property.

Also, when you go to sell (if you ever sell), your single-family home, you will also have the widest field of potential buyers. First, you will have other investors who could purchase your rental to add to their investment portfolio (especially if there is a great tenant already in it). Then you will also of course have the wider population of home buyers simply looking to purchase the property as a home to live in themselves.

Another advantage to single-family homes as rentals, especially 3-bedroom homes, is that the tenants that are most attracted to this type of property are typically families. Once a family moves into a home as your tenant, a house simply feels like "home." You don't have anyone sharing a wall with you, you very likely have your own yard, and it's simply easier emotionally for a family to "settle in." Add in the fact that your tenant's kids can get used to the local schools, etc., and it is very common for single-family homes to stay rented to the same family for a long time. Of course, this isn't guaranteed, but by the nature of families as tenants, your tenant turnover rate could be far less than in a muti-unit apartment-style property.

Lastly, another major advantage to single-family homes as rentals is that there are no utilities to "split" (or simply absorb because they aren't split). Since there is only one tenant renting the entire property, the full electric bill, the full water bill, etc. is automatically going to be your tenant's full responsibility. It is also very common and reasonable to arrange that your tenant will have to do their own lawn mowing and/or snow removal, etc.

The Advantages of Multi-Family Homes:

The first advantage of Multi-Family homes is what is called "Economies of Scale." With a duplex, triplex, or 4-plex, you would have one roof to maintain for multiple tenants' homes, one lawn for multiple tenants' homes, etc. So, the cost of doing repairs is scaled and spread over multiple tenants' rental income, and may have less of an impact on your total revenue for the year.

Along this same idea is the safety of your rental income because that too is spread over multiple tenants and it is unlikely that all of your tenants will move out at the same time! So, if one tenant moves out, you will likely still have income coming in from the rest of your tenants. In a single-family home, of course, if your one and only tenant moves out, you have zero income until they are replaced.

For these reasons, the math on multi-unit properties almost always work out better on paper. I say "on paper" however, because in all cases, every property must be analyzed individually. Multi-family properties are seen more as "apartments" than they are "homes"- so speaking very generally, it may not be families that rent from you - it may be younger single people, couples, or even retired older people. In the case of younger single people, they tend to move more often than a family settling into a place they call home. So, you have to be more comfortable with tenant turnover.

Also - you have to pay very close attention to utilities - because not every building has separate meters for every utility to every tenant. For this reason, a lot of amateur landlords simply decide to pay utilities rather than to try to argue over which tenant owes what. If one of the utilities you as the property owner would have to pay is the heating bill for an entire building in a cold climate – that could kill your profits right there!

Even if every unit does have separate utility metering, you as the property owner will likely also have your own utility meter for "common areas." Exterior landscaping maintenance and watering, snow removal, trash, lighting of parking areas and walkways will all likely be your responsibility because how could you possibly split the cost with the tenants without a riot ("I don't even use the lawn – arrrr!"). You'd just have to include it in the rent you charge.

Now, a badly managed property with issues like huge non-separately-metered utility bills honestly represents an opportunity for a savvy investor to correct them and increase the rental income by doing so - so I'm not saying steer clear at all costs - but this would be a bit of an advanced thing to take on as your first rental property – don't you think? Maybe not. In any case, just be aware of potential issues like this and look out for them.

So, I think you get the idea. There are, in fact, pros and cons to a single-family home as your first rental vs. a multi-unit - with strong advantages and disadvantages on both sides. I think the tie-breaker here is to keep in mind that this is your first rental property - not your last. If you feel stuck thinking too hard here, or you have fear about one or the other type of property - then cross it off your list and go with what is comfortable enough for you to take action on now. Taking action, at the end of the day, is going to be what makes you an investor. Remember - your real learning begins *after* your first property.

My Personal Opinion

My goal is to educate you to make your own choices, not persuade you into ours, but I do want to provide my personal take on this issue. I think you should start with a 3-bedroom, single family home. Period.

Multi-family homes might be tempting, but you have enough "new" things to digest emotionally and intellectually. You're going to be building a team, etc. and doing a lot of new things for the first time. There will be enough pushing you out of your comfort zone, so leaving the physical property itself as something in your comfort zone would be wise. If you get bored quickly with single-family rentals – great! That means you've nailed it and you are ready to get more advanced. No harm. But biting off more than you can chew and having a bad first experience could be devastating financially and emotionally.

Along with my advice to purchase a 3-bedroom, single-family home as your first rental, is to avoid the temptation to get any "odd-ball" houses just because they are in a "good area" or a "great price." If every house on the street is 3-bedroom, and you purchase the only 2-bedroom…yikes! It may have been cheaper to buy, but how much difference did that price really make on your mortgage payment? Now you have to charge much lower rent, and families won't likely be your tenants.

I'm not saying to never buy a 2-bedroom. Maybe there's a row of 2-bedroom houses that a property manager has a waiting list for because they are walking distance to a major hospital and shopping and so retirees love them. Just know that you are now departing from the mainstream into a niche – and I don't suggest small niches for your first rental.

Also, even within 3-bedroom homes, make sure your property "conforms" to what is normal in that neighborhood. If every other house has a 2-car garage, yours had better have a 2-car garage. If every other house has a decently-sized, fenced yard, yours had better have a decently-sized, fenced yard. In life, there are lots of times when being unique is great – but with your first rental property – blend in, and give your customer, who are the tenants in that area and price range – what they are looking for!

Lastly, avoid the temptation of purchasing a "fixer" house as your first rental. I don't mind if a house needs "paint and carpet" or maybe new appliances – all of which your property manager can help arrange for you, but don't get into a major rehab project. There's just enough going on right now without adding another major element to the mix. In the "advanced" version of this book I may write next, sure, but let's leave rehabs alone for now.

What about Condo's?

In the next chapter I will discuss a concept called "House Hacking" which basically means moving out of a property you already currently live in and turning it into your first rental property. If the home you currently live in is a Condo, or a Townhouse, or even a Single-Family Home that is part of a "Planned Urban Development" and so it has a Home Owners Association, then it may be beneficial to you to analyze your current residence as a potential rental using the deal-analysis methods taught later in the book.

If we are starting from scratch, however, and can pick from any available property as our first rental, I really don't like condo's in general simply because of the restrictions you are living under as part of your Home Owners Association (HOA). Your HOA will tell you everything that you can, and can't do with your condo – including if you can even rent it out at all.

There is also pretty much nothing you can do to the outside of a condo or townhome to make it more appealing to tenants – it just is what it is – you usually can't paint the exterior of the property or landscape the property to enhance the "curb appeal" whatsoever. But – unlike me, you may see this lack of control as an advantage because the HOA is responsible for maintaining the exterior, etc.

So, I can't say never have a condo as a rental property, all I can say is don't ignore the analysis – look out for deferred maintenance and the overall financial health of your HOA, and what restrictions may befall you as you rent your own property out. Condo investing may be your thing – and I wish you the best - I just can't be the one to lead you there.

Final Thoughts

I listen to a lot of successful investors tell their stories, and a theme I see over and over is that despite what they are investing in now, a large number of them got their start with single family homes. In fact, one of the most famous teachers on the subject of Cash-Flow will herself tell a story of a two-bedroom home she purchased as a first rental - with her hands shaking from nervousness as she signed the purchase agreement! Today, her and her very famous husband have hundreds, if not thousands of rental units, mostly in large apartment complexes.

Most successful investors give a large amount of credit to their humble beginnings and the confidence it gave them as investors, which ultimately un-locked the journey they took to be who they are today. My wife and I certainly feel that way. I mention it so that you are not anxious as you gain experience. Again, if you're quickly bored with your first rental, you're doing it right. At that point, with a team, and increased confidence, see where you want to go from there. Is one rental enough? Do you want more single-family homes given their simplicity? Or, do you want more advanced multi-family projects? You'll know what's right for you as your *second* deal when you get there – so let's get you there!

Chapter 10:

How Much Property Can I Afford?

Your Mortgage Broker is going to walk you through everything you could ever want to know regarding financing your rental property. Still, it is helpful to have some general guidelines in mind so you know what to prepare for.

When you are purchasing a home to live in for yourself, lenders call this "Owner-Occupied Property" - and they see mortgages on these homes as less of a risk because generally speaking people are going to fight and do whatever they can to pay the mortgage on their own home and not lose the house they live in.

On the other hand, when you are purchasing a property specifically to rent it out to someone else - this is called "Non-Owner-Occupied Property" and it is considered more of a risk because, after all, you don't live there and if things get tough there is less incentive to fight to make the mortgage payment. At least that's the theory.

So, for non-owner-occupied property, like the rental property you are going to be purchasing, lenders want to see a much higher down payment than if you were simply buying a home for yourself to live in. As I write this, these are the current down-payment requirements for rental investment property:

For a Single-Family Home (a typical house) as a rental property, you are likely going to be asked for a 20% down-payment. So, if you are buying a $100,000 house, your down payment will be $20,000.

For a 2 to 4 Unit / Multi-Unit Property as a rental (often called a Duplex, Triplex, or 4-Plex/Quad-Plex), you are going to need a 25% down-payment. So, if you are buying a $100,000 property, your down payment will be $25,000.

Now, keep in mind that a down payment is not the only cost involved in purchasing a property. You will need "closing costs" that your mortgage broker can explain – as well as the cost of home inspections, etc. you are going to want to perform that your Realtor can explain.

Interest rates and lending guidelines are always changing, but knowing current rates to use in your analysis is not a problem - because your mortgage broker is just a quick email or phone call away to talk through any purchasing ideas you may have! They will know the current reality on all of these costs, which is why I am not going to try to specifically estimate them here - except to say that if you figure in another 3-5% of the purchase price of the home for these costs you should be close enough to not be devastated when you hear the real numbers from your mortgage broker.

"House-Hacking"

This book is written for the vast majority of us that will be purchasing a rental property specifically to rent it out from day 1. However, there are a couple of other circumstances that may or may not apply to you – and may or may not appeal to you – that you should know about that may allow you to "hack" your way into a rental property a slightly different way.

Specifically, if you are lucky enough to live in an area that is also a great area for rental property, you may consider purchasing a home to live in as your Primary Residence for a period of time, and then turn it into a rental property later. This would allow you to put substantially far less as a down payment. Just be totally up-front with your mortgage broker about this idea so he can guide you on the restrictions and timelines you will have to follow to avoid mortgage fraud! Yes, that's a real thing. You can't pretend to live in a house yourself when it's really going to be a rental. But, after you've lived in the house a certain period of time, it's totally fine to do so. Again, your mortgage broker will guide you.

Your CPA will also tell you how your taxes will change when you do make the switch-over to making your own home a rental. If this does end up being a viable option for you – be sure to run a full analysis of the property as a rental before you purchase it to live in for a while (as you will be taught to do later in this book). Keep in mind that since you are putting far less down so your mortgage payment will be higher – make sure the numbers work!

But even if the numbers are close, and the cash-flow is a bit of a "squeaker" - keep in mind, that assuming you have a fixed interest-rate, your mortgage payment will stay the same for 30 years – however, your rental income will likely ratchet-up with inflation. Eventually, as your cash-flow grows, why not pretend that income isn't even there and simply put it as an extra payment on top of your mortgage? What if by doing so, in 20 years you have a paid-off rental house (you used to live in). What would just that one move, one time, do for your retirement? Perhaps you prefer a rental nearby even if the return is less, and if this comfort gets you in the game – go for it!

House-Hacking Twist

Another rental property "hack" might be that perhaps you are in a place in life that you really wouldn't mind living in an apartment – if you owned the building! If this is you, perhaps you can purchase a 2, 3, or 4-unit property, live in one of the units and rent out the others. Again, your mortgage broker will tell you what advantages there may be to living in your own rental property – and, of course, loop in your CPA into the discussion as early as possible as well.

Just keep in mind – when you move out of your personal residence and turn it into a rental, everything changes about that property – you will need different insurance, you will have different tax advantages to follow and understand, and you may wish to change title of the property into a legal entity such as an LLC for protection of your other assets – all of which is discussed elsewhere in this book.

Sources of Purchase Money:

Here is a list of memory-joggers for possible sources of purchase money you may have…

1) Personal Savings (obviously).
2) An old IRA / 401k (yes, you can use this for real estate ask your CPA about the in's and out's).
3) A loan from a current 401k.
4) Refinance your own home and take cash out.
5) A home-equity line of credit from your own home.
6) Cash Value inside Life Insurance (Cash out or loan against it).
7) Refinance a paid-off car, pulling cash out.
8) Personal Loans from a bank or even a friend that wouldn't mind lending money to you, especially if it was secured by real estate or other collateral you may have.
9) Partners! Why not! Share a learning curve and the costs! (By the way, partnering with a friend is how I did my very first rental years ago before I was married). Just make sure you are both completely on-board with the journey ahead and the outcome you expect – whatever it is, you both have to agree.
10) Credit cards! While you won't be able to put your down payment itself on a credit card – you can actually charge things like the loan appraisal, property inspection, and even work to prep the rental that you and your property manager have determined are needed like perhaps a new stove, etc.

Now - the question of how much property you can afford is different than how much property you *should* afford. Currently, bread-and-butter, 3-bedroom homes that are in great, working-class neighborhoods (we will discuss neighborhoods later) can be found in many major cities for around $100,000 to $150,000 (don't worry if you don't live in one of those cities! We will teach you about long-distance investing later).

Now, if instead of one of these more desirable $100,000 properties, right now you can only afford a $60,000 property in a bad area - don't compromise your standards! Wait and save up more money or find a partner. Likewise, if you can afford a much nicer home, perhaps that costs $200,000 or more - don't just automatically buy it. Keep an investor's eye - do the analysis you are going to be learning later in this book - and see where the "sweet spot" is in terms of area quality, home price, rental income, and your personal comfort zone. Making a car analogy - you may find that there is more profit to be made purchasing a Toyota to rent out instead of a Mercedes Benz, while equally comfortable to you as an investor. Hold this thought as we proceed...

Chapter 11:

What "Neighborhood Type" Should I Purchase a Rental Property In?

Once you've decided on a property size - you must now decide on a neighborhood "type." This may seem like an odd question - I mean, wouldn't you want a "nice" neighborhood? Well, yes - but think about buying a car...obviously you want a reliable car - but that can mean a lot of things.... Do you want a Toyota or a Mercedes? A pickup truck or a sports car? All reliable cars will get you there - but the driving experience is going to be very different. This is also true for the investing experience of different neighborhood types.

Inside professional investing, there is an un-official, but commonly-used, "A-B-C-D-F" grading system when it comes to neighborhoods. Yes, A is the nicest neighborhood, and F is the worst in terms of the wealth it takes to live there - but, as you will see, by no means does that mean that as investors we automatically want an "A" neighborhood for our rentals. Let's get some basic understanding of these neighborhood types, and then we can discuss them together.

Now, please keep in mind - every city has every neighborhood type. What changes is the price range for each type based on the city. For example, in Los Angeles, a $250,000 home, if you can find one, would be in a D or F neighborhood. The same $250,000 in parts of the Mid-West or South would get you into a very strong B or perhaps even an A neighborhood.

"A" Neighborhoods

"A" Neighborhoods are the upper-end of housing in any given city. They are where doctors, lawyers, and other higher-income people live. The cars in the driveways will be names like Lexus, Mercedes, Infiniti, etc. For reference, if you know it, in Southern California you'd be talking about Beverly Hills, Santa Monica, Sierra Madre, Newport Beach, Etc. In Indiana, this would be suburbs of Indianapolis like Carmel. A-areas will have restaurants with little twinkly lights and white table cloths.

One might think that A Neighborhoods are the best ones for rentals but that isn't necessarily the case. That is because often times the purchase price for these properties can often be so high, that even with rent also being higher than other areas, the rental income still isn't quite enough to make the numbers make sense. (We will be discussing how to analyze a rental property shortly).

"B" Neighborhoods

"B" Neighborhoods are still very clean, but they are where more everyday people live and work. People that live in these neighborhoods have a blend of "White Collar" jobs and skilled "Blue Collar" jobs. Here, you'll find nurses, cops, teachers, retail store managers, etc. In fact, my wife and I live in this type of neighborhood. The cars in the driveways are fairly-new Hondas, Chevy's, Fords, Toyotas, or SUV/Pickup Trucks that are in great shape.

Kids stay in B Neighborhoods to trick-or-treat on Halloween and you'll see kids riding their bikes. Just about all of the lawns are mowed, the houses are in great condition, there aren't any spare/strange cars lying around and there's no graffiti that lingers without being removed quickly. There is crime, but it is unlikely to be violent crime. Car thefts, etc. can happen anywhere, but a B Neighborhood will be easily and quickly regarded as a "good" area by the average person. Being near public transportation is not crucially important as most families will have a car. But - being near good schools might be. B-areas will have restaurants like Applebee's and Olive Garden.

Potential renters for your B-area property are usually going to be working families, who are generally fairly stable financially. You may also like the intangible peace of mind of being able to tell yourself "My B-area rental house is cute and on a nice street." This emotional reassurance from your own eyes liking the property you have selected can be a huge factor in keeping your blood pressure low as you venture into investing - especially if you need to invest long-distance. My wife and I invest in B Neighborhoods, and if B Neighborhoods make you comfortable enough to get in the game then don't worry if a property doesn't exactly conform to the 1% Rule. So long as the numbers are reasonable to you, and you're comfortable with the property and the area, then I'd say just get in the game!

"C" Neighborhoods

"C" Neighborhoods are where more "Blue Collar" workers live. Here you'll find the cashier at the retail store, the restaurant worker, the plumber, factory worker, janitor, mechanic, etc. C-areas are by no means "bad" areas. They are where regular, hard-working people live. C-areas may have some lawns that aren't mowed, but that might just be because a resident is a renter and the amateur landlord hasn't bothered to keep up the property. In C-areas you'll see some cars that don't run, but a C-area is *not* the "hood" or a "dangerous" place to be.

Being close to public transportation is more important in C-areas as it's possible that not every family, or everyone in the family, has their own car. Cars might be the same as in a B-area in terms of brand and style, but they will likely be a bit older. Restaurants in a C-area might be more fast-food, but you'll see some Denny's-style, affordable family restaurants as well.

"C" Neighborhoods are the favorite of many professional investors. This is because rents in a C-area are usually are stronger relative to the purchase price of the property (as per 1% Rule). For example, you might find a $80,000 house in a C-area that rents for $900, and a mile away is a $120,000 house in a B area that rents for $1,100 – so on paper, the C-area home would be a stronger rental performer relative to price.

Also, some investors like C-areas because they are "improving" and aside from cash-flow, the investor is speculating that the area might become a B-area eventually, at which point property values may increase. This is especially true if there is new economic development or a new large employer coming into a C-area. My wife and I would absolutely invest in the right "C" opportunity.

But – again, the numbers are just one aspect of the deal. Talk to your property manager and determine the trade-offs to a C-area vs. a B-area. Ask, for example, if it's harder to get tenants to stay a long time, etc. Really balance out the equation in your mind considering all aspects of the property and make sure it all makes sense to you. I can only speak in generalities here, but you and your property manager can really drill down to what advantages and disadvantages exist in your local area of investing focus. That is exactly what your team is for.

Personal Side-Note

Whether we are talking about B-areas or C-areas - these areas are always going to be in the most demand by both renters and buyers because they are in a zone where people are always moving up into - and down into. It is the middle, center-cut of the pot roast called American neighborhoods. (wow - a food analogy - I usually make car analogies - maybe I'm getting hungry).

When I did my first rental with a best friend years ago it was in a C-area, and my wife and I would have no problem investing in the right C-area opportunity today. In fact, on the lower-B/higher-C border are some great, optimized opportunities in terms of the 1% Rule and area condition (as your trained eye will soon be able to spot). Please know, also, my wife and I did pick a B-area for our first long-distance rental – it just felt nice and that gave us comfort since we would be living far away. There's no wrong answer so long as your eyes are wide open to all of the pros and cons.

"D" Neighborhoods

D-areas are officially a bit sketchy. You might have a few well-kept homes, but then there will be homes that are boarded up on the same street, and nobody seems to be in a hurry to fix them. D-areas will also typically have more uncut lawns and deferred maintenance. You will also see more people simply walking around because they may not have a car (or anything to do all day?). Graffiti is visible, and some trash may have been dumped in the alleys or curbsides. Some investors may like D-areas if they are specializing on "Section 8" (government-subsidized) housing, or if they are betting on the city dumping money into redevelopment of that area and they are hoping this area turns into the next "art's community" or similar area with rising property values.

Also, some investors can be allured by what - on paper - may be a tremendous return on investment (they think) by looking at the rental income compared to the very low price of the property. However, factor in the financial stability of the tenant pool, and the turnover, damage, vacancy, or evictions you might face, and sorry – D-areas are a "pass" for us. This type of area may really speak to you however, which is fine. Just know that you are a bit of a pioneer and speculator in a D-area, and you will face the potential risks and rewards of being so. Again, for us, the power of rental real estate is the known, present performance of an area without any speculation of improvement, and D-areas don't pass that test.

"F" Neighborhoods

Professional investors affectionally refer to F-areas as "war zones." They are below D-areas in that they are known gang areas, crime hotbeds, or abandoned areas, and, well… Unless you are a huge speculator, "F" simply means "Forget about it."

I have a best friend that lives in a strong B area now, but once upon a time he had rentals in F areas. He still tells stories about collecting rent in-person with a gun in his pocket. He also told me stories about a tenant that would simply throw trash out the kitchen window instead of taking it out to the curb. Um, yea…I'm out.

I can already hear some of you saying "yea, but…" questions, and the answer is no! lol. When you are in a position to purchase an entire inner-city apartment building and offer it to a local homeless shelter free of cost, then I hope you do so. God will bless us so that we can bless others.

Final Thoughts

While we should always do our business charitably, we owe it to the world to run a real business so that we have the financial capacity to do real charity. By trying to run a business as a charity, it is highly likely you will not be doing much business or much charity in the end. Providing great service to hard working tenants that deserve a great place to live for a reasonable cost with a highly responsive manager is plenty to offer. Keep the rest as pure charity to the needy.

Chapter 12:

What City Should I Invest In?

With the 1% Rule firmly in our minds, and some general sense of what neighborhood types are, it is time to look at what city can match your personal criteria you are developing as you digest your options.

Of course, the first place to begin the search for your first rental property is in your own city. Keep in mind that a great rental property doesn't have to be in an area you would like to live personally. If you've decided you want to invest in a single-family home in a B-area, and there's a great B-area all the way across town far from your job, that's ok. It's close to your tenant's job, and that's the point!

The next place to search are suburbs of your city, and then also widen the search and take a look at reasonably-sized cities within a day's drive of where you live. You may find a great neighborhood pocket you had never considered before.

Start the Search Online

Pop open Zillow.com and set the settings to show properties for sale and for rent at the same time. Scan around on the map until you find pockets that conform to the 1% Rule. Next, of course, ask yourself if these properties are in a price range you could realistically afford? If so, continue further...

Click through on the actual individual property listings showing up on Zillow.com and take a look at what type and quality of property they are. (I also love the website Redfin.com to look at property listings if they serve the city you are looking in). Once you click through and actually see the listing of the properties for sale in that neighborhood pocket - ask yourself - are they newer? Older? In good shape? Do they appeal to you as an investor? If so, continue further...

Next, click over to maps.google.com. Put in a property address from one of the listings, and click through to "Street View." I'm sure you may be familiar with this feature, but if not, this in an incredible feature that allows you to virtually "tour" a neighborhood. Click the arrows to "walk" up and down the street the potential rental property is on. What kind of neighborhood is it? What kind of cars are in the driveways? What condition are the houses and front yards in? (You will be able to tell what year the photos were taken so keep that in mind as well – but Google keeps things pretty recent). Do you like what you see? If so, continue further…

Keep "walking" on maps.google.com until you hit a major intersection nearby, what's on the major corners? Gas stations? Liquor Stores? What kind of shopping is nearby? Any notable schools or hospitals? Are there basic amenities nearby like Grocery Stores, or a Target or Wal-Mart? What about public transportation lines? (Keep in mind, you may personally love "trendy" restaurants or stores to be nearby where you live, but if you are investing in a B or C area, it would be much more important to have the basics nearby in terms of shopping and necessities).

At this point, you should have an idea if this is an A, B, C, D, or F area. Now, ask yourself if this area seems to meet your criteria for your first rental property? If so, take note of the area, and the particular property in question….then go to www.Realtor.com – put in the property address, and find the actual listing agent of that property (Zillow or Redfin will replace that agent with their own agent on their website). Take note of that agent's contact info – because guess what – after we double check just a couple of more things about the area - now you just may have one of the three Realtor's you are going to reach out to and interview for your team!

Personal Side Note:

For us, we look for areas that meet the 1% Rule, are B or C areas, with 3-bedroom, single-family homes that are going for about $100,000. You are more than welcome to follow in our footsteps –

but whatever criteria speaks to you, when you find properties, and a neighborhood that fit it – put them on a list! There is still more homework to do, but at least you have an area to start looking in more closely. At this point, keep searching – how many areas that meet your criteria can you find?

Analyze the Area

Let's say you've found a zip code or two with neighborhood pockets that seem to meet your investing criteria. Maybe you've even found a specific property or two you like and you're almost ready to call the Realtor's offering them for sale to interview for your team. Before you do, it's time to get a better sense of the economic and population trends in that area. To do this, go to www.city-data.com

This is a great website that compiles data on every city or zip code. Simply enter the City or Zip code and you can suddenly see the population growth trends, employment trends, household income, etc. I also like to do some Google searches as well, such as: "Major Employers in (your target city)." "Crime Map of (your target city)."

What I'm really looking for is this: I want to see a city where the population is growing. I want to see a city where there are multiple major employers. I don't want a dying city where people are moving away, and there is one big factory that everyone works in, and if that shuts down then literally everyone is unemployed! This is a real thing! In other words - does this city have it going on? Can real people move here, live here, and afford it here? If so, it should be a great place for rentals.

If you are researching a major city – this is easy to determine by looking at the population and employment data, but if you are looking in a suburb of a city, keep something else in mind as well: Can residents of that suburb easily commute to jobs in the main heart of the city? If so, it is less important that the suburb have its own "Economic Base," meaning local employers, etc. If residents of a suburb can drive 20 minutes to a job in the major city nearby, it's ok if the suburb is a bit quaint and doesn't have a lot of business activity. If, however, the suburb is 30, or 40 minutes away from a major city, then it had better have its own jobs! So, in that case run the data for that suburb / smaller city and see if it can stand on its own economically.

Again, a property manager and Realtor with local knowledge will ultimately help you draw the line. Just don't automatically fall in love with, or dismiss, an area that seems a bit outside of a major city. It could be a place people prefer to live and then just commute into the city for work. You just have to look closer to know for sure. But all of this analysis is just part of the screening process – and it's all happening from your laptop while you're sitting in bed!

So, at this point – if an area is still passing your test, go ahead and reach out to those Realtors and start building your team!

Before you Buy

Once your team is built and you are really getting close to pulling the trigger on a particular property, there is a little deeper analysis you need to do – even if it doesn't sway your decision to buy or now, it's just good stuff to know…. This includes:

Check the Schools

I would say to do the same Google search for school rankings just to make sure that you know the school rankings in your potential property's area. Regardless of the outcome, I'd only be excited or concerned if the rankings you find for your property's area are especially good, or especially bad *relative* to other similar areas. You don't want to be in the only area with bad schools but you do want to be able to sell the fact that your house is near the best schools.

Otherwise, however, if you are in a city where the schools are relatively the same everywhere, it really doesn't matter quite as much. Remember, if you are looking at rentals in B and C areas, these are working families living regular lives. These families, like myself, want clean, comfortable, safe places to live, work, learn, and play. We're not trying to sell an upscale "A" neighborhood buyer on the top-ranked, nationally acclaimed school down the street. In some cities, frankly all the schools are "meh" - we just want to make sure we're not buying into the only "dog" school area in town.

Check the Buzz

Whatever neighborhood you are looking in likely has an official name you can see on the map, or at least an unofficial nickname known to locals. Sometimes, a neighborhood will simply be known as "south of the freeway," etc. So, however the area is known, I would Google the city and that neighborhood name and see what comes up. I've found that a lot of chat rooms and message boards exist for people looking to relocate to a city, and there are always a ton of locals posting their opinions of different neighborhoods. Take it with a grain of salt, but, if you start seeing good, or bad, comments over and over, you can be there's something to them. Also, your search may reveal an article or two about developments or improvements planned in the area.

Check the City Planning Office

You might be amazed how friendly and willing to talk people are that work in the City Planning office of a particular city (especially a smaller city). You can call and ask what plans for improvements might be on the drawing board for certain areas that wouldn't be obvious just driving down the street. If you find out the city doesn't have anything particular planned for your area, that's not necessarily bad news. Most "redevelopment" plans are for areas that need improving. This type of information would be more important to you if you were planning to invest in C or, gulp, D areas and the area improving in the future is a big part of your strategy.

It's fun making a connection at a City Planning office. You learn a lot of neat stuff. Like, for example, there is an older/historic suburb of Indianapolis where we like fishing for rentals – and there are a lot of houses listed for sale built in the year "1900." When I was talking to the local planner I happened to mention

"Wow, 1900 was really a big year for construction," and the planner laughed – she told me, "No, what happens is that if we don't actually know what year a house was built we just list it as 1900." Haha! I love it - that's called local knowledge!

So, without even leaving home you have explored your neighborhood, your state, or even other states, and you have found a few target areas to start building a team in. How cool is that!

Chapter 13:

Investing Long-Distance

Assuming you've done the online search outlined in the previous chapter and there's nothing remotely close to where you live that will work as your first rental. Well, then join the club! Haha...

If this whole time you have been wondering where the heck people are finding investment properties for $100,000 because where you live that price doesn't exist - then you are not alone. Aunt Laura had the privilege of investing in her own neighborhood 40 years ago. But today – nothing cash-flows in the state where we live (and Aunt Laura lived), let alone the city.

The good news, however, is that there are large sections of the country where finding rental properties that will work great is very common. In case you are still wondering - my wife and I live in California and invest in the Mid-West. We have flown out there many times and have built great relationships in our travels. Building a team long-distance really isn't any different than building one locally. Either way, it all starts online or by phone anyway – so please don't get intimidated.

And you know what - that's actually a very liberating thing to embrace the fact that we have to invest long distance, because - once you have to get on a plane to find a great place to invest, it's really all the same - so why not pick a great place for rentals wherever it may be...and a fun city you want to visit on your big adventure!

Attention Californian's!
(and other coastal, big-city folk...)

Planning your next vacation? Consider an exotic destination where...Everyone's nice!...It's Inexpensive!
And...you already speak the language!

It's called...***America!***

A Tale of Two Americas...

Take a look at the two houses above… the first one is the actual house my wife and I live in today in California. It's a small, yellow-ish, 3-bedroom house, on a large lot, it's fairly cute, and it's on a nice street.

If we were going to purchase this house on the open market at the time this book is being written, it would cost us about $500,000.

Now, take a look at the house below it... it's an actual house my wife and I purchased as a rental property in Indianapolis, Indiana. It's a small, yellow-ish, 3-bedroom house, on a large lot, it's fairly cute, and it's on a nice street.

If we were going to purchase this house on the open market at the time this book is being written, it would cost us under $100,000. (Similar selections of even larger houses could range from only $125,000 - $150,000).

Now, the price of the Indiana house may come as a shock to most Californians, New Yorkers, etc. - who are used to their cars costing that much. But, as amazing as the price is, the miracle of the Indiana house isn't even the low price - instead, is the rent you can get *relative* to the price of the house. (Remember the 1% Rule).

For example, let's look at both houses, and compare the price of the house to the percentage of the price you can receive in monthly rent:

	California House:	Indiana House:
Purchase Price:	$500,000	$90,000
Monthly Rent:	$2,500	$900
Percentage %:	**0.5%**	**1.0%**

While the California House costs nearly *six times* as much as the Indiana House, it only gets a little better than *three times* the rent. Just with this very basic math, there seems like there might be an opportunity with the Indiana house when it comes to Cash-Flow, because you can simply rent out the Indiana house for much more *relative* to its purchase price.

I already covered earlier how to explore and search for possible cities for rentals, and building a team is the same process anywhere. If you have to go long-distance to find areas that work for rentals, don't lose heart - there are actually *advantages* to this I will discuss next...

Advantages of Long-Distance Investing

Believe it or not, I actually think there are advantages to long-distance investing. The largest advantage is that you are forced to be an investor - not a landlord. You couldn't micro-manage your rental property even if you wanted to! You *have* to have a team!

For that reason, you will not be tempted to do things yourself - instead, you will unleash your mind and your capabilities from day 1. Once you can invest long-distance, the entire country becomes your playground. You get to travel and see new places and meet new people! Your "vacations" to visit your property, meet your team, and explore new areas become business tax write-offs (talk to your CPA), and the entire process is invigorating. To do this efficiently - here is what I suggest:

Get as far as you can online and over the phone in terms of finding a city, and building a team. Make sure you have a real connection to at least a Realtor, and that you genuinely like the thought of visiting a city. At that point – it's time to plan a trip!

Make a trip or two over a few months to meet your team, and get to know a few areas of town you really like. Be there hands-on for your first rental property purchase. Then, with a trusted team in place, and having personally visited those areas of town, you should eventually get to the point that you are comfortable purchasing property you haven't necessarily personally seen. This means you get to fly back again when (and if) you want, not necessarily to examine each deal.

Remember - once you build relationships you get to enjoy them forever. Once you understand a city you get to enjoy it forever. You will find and get to know your favorite restaurant - you will have "your thing" you like to do when you visit there. If you have family in other areas of the country - take a look around where they live for investment opportunities. Then flying back to visit them and your property can happen at the same time. Make it fun - make it an adventure. With national banks you can move money easily and with the internet everything else is a breeze. Don't fear long-distance investing if rental real estate is in your heart. You'll know when things are serious enough for you to get on a plane. Make it happen.

Picking a Long-Distance City

All of the rules for picking a city covered earlier still apply in long-distance investing, but where do you begin your long-distance search to even know what cities to analyze?

Ok, so say we're starting from scratch in picking a city - we have no friends, or business connections anywhere we can use as a starting point. Well, then here's how I'd start (keep in mind once you have picked a city and built a team, you can invest there happily for years and years so don't be intimidated by the process).

Google some Articles

To just get your juices flowing, start by Googling some articles on "Best cities for real estate investors in 2020" (or whatever the year is), or, "Best rental markets in (this year)." Now, keep in mind, a lot of these articles will be focused on appreciation, not necessarily cash-flow as rental investment, but still - take a look at the list. You will also find a mix of actual articles by journalists, as well as marketing "articles" from people who sell turn-key investments (I will discuss later) but it's all good for right now - just start seeing what city names start popping up.

Continue Googling, but this time search for something like "most livable cities (this year)," "most affordable cities (this year)," "cities most people are moving to (this year)," "best cities for first-time home buyers," "best cities for jobs growth," etc. While the search results will certainly vary with time, you are likely to see cities pop up in the "heartland" - Texas, Indiana, Ohio, etc. But again, things change with time.

Look at the Suburbs

Very often when a city is popular for investors, there are suburbs of the main city that get overlooked, but that are just as great of an opportunity. Don't be afraid of a smaller city within the same state – or even suburb of a city that is perhaps 15-20 minutes away from a larger city - a lot of people would be willing to commute to the big city to work, and then come home to a quieter town. In these cases, we want to make sure the large city the suburb is near is strong in terms of employment and population growth. Remember, if a suburb is more than 20-30 minutes from a major city, however, that smaller town might still be a great opportunity for investment - but in that case I would want to evaluate that town on its stand-alone economic strength.

Don't Worry About Being Trendy

One of the greatest aspects of rental real estate investing is that it really isn't very glamorous or fast-paced. If a city or a suburb catches your eye that does not appear in any article or on any "hot list" - don't worry! Just be sure to qualify the city with your criteria, and if it passes the test - and you like the city - then go for it! People live, work, and pay rent everywhere!

Personal Note

Right now, for our next rental acquisition, we are continuing to explore Indiana as well as new opportunities through new relationships with Realtors I've developed in Oklahoma, and Texas. But there are a lot of cities that look great on paper – and most of them are in the Mid-West, and South. If there's a city that piques your interest for whatever reason, go through the online search criteria we've just discussed and maybe you will find a great pocket nobody's looking at (remember, boring is great when it comes to rental property).

Make a Top-3 List

Make a list of perhaps 3 cities or suburbs of cities that catch your eye, and let's go onto the next step of getting even deeper into analysis… (refer back to Chapter 11 *What City Should I Invest In?* to continue to process of analyzing the health of a city). If it passes that test, it's time to pick up the phone and start building a team!

Tie-Breaker

If at this point you are finding more than one City that meet your criteria, how do you break the tie? I would say to pick the City you actually feel you would like to visit more than the other as a tourist. Maybe there's a museum, a sports facility, a natural landmark, an art's scene, a micro-brewery, or any other local draw to you that you would actually enjoy visiting. Other Cities can stay on your list for later, but first go where it would be fun to go. This first property is an "educational adventure" as much as it is an investment. Have fun with it, and start tasting the lifestyle of an investor as you work/travel/play all at the same time.

Also, as you start reaching out and building a team, if you feel a really great connection to a real estate agent or property manager you feel can really help you – can that relationship alone break a tie? Yes! Relationships are everything in this business, and don't be afraid to factor them in heavily in your decision to pick one similarly-qualified city over another for your first rental. In doing so, you will not only have found a new team member, you will likely also have made a new friend and tour guide. My wife and I go eat Indian food and play miniature golf with our property manager and her family every time we visit. She has become a true friend that has enriched our lives personally and as investors.

So, you – while still sitting on your couch at home – have at this point found a city that looks promising for rentals, and have even found a few listed for sale that seem to conform to the 1% Rule... Now it's time for some detailed analysis, so let's learn how!

PART 5

RENTAL PROPERTY DEAL ANALYSIS

Chapter 14:

How Do I Analyze a Rental Property?

The math is simple!

There - I had to say that first, because I know some of you are afraid of math like I used to be, and so you may only read the first line of this chapter - so I wanted to make it count!

To do a rental property analysis, all we need to know are three things:

1) What are your *Acquisition Costs?* (This is the total cost we are going to spend acquiring this property).

2) What is the total *Rental Income* we can expect from this property?

3) What are your *Monthly Expenses* in operating this property?

After that, we subtract our expenses from our income and hopefully we are left with a monthly profit. That monthly profit is called *Cash Flow*. You'll see this as we go along, just know this is simple!

So, keeping that simplicity in mind, let's go through the details of how to add all of this up.... As we go along – please just focus on the particular numbers of that section of the analysis – don't worry that you're not "keeping it all straight" – we will put it all together in the end. For now, let's just get the numbers.

Quick note: keep in mind that for now, we will largely be using "place holder estimates" that are reasonable numbers based on what things generally cost. Once you are further along in actually acquiring a particular property, you can replace these estimates with actual, precise figures your team will be giving you. For example, we will replace our estimate on insurance costs with an actual quote from your insurance agent, etc. But, doing this initial analysis should get you very close, especially if you are conservative in your numbers. I'm also going to use an example property that conforms to the 1% Rule perfectly just as a baseline.

So, as above, the first group of figures to calculate is the full Acquisition Cost of the property... So, either in Excel, or on a napkin, or however you wish, write down the following numbers (I'm assuming a property costing $100,000 for my example figures but your team will tell you the exact numbers):

1. Acquisition Costs Include:

1) <u>Your Down-Payment for the property</u> - (Example 20%, which means $20,000 for a $100,000 property) *Your Mortgage Broker will give you the exact number - assume 20% down for now.*

2) <u>Loan and Title Closing Costs</u> - (Example $3,000). *You will get this exact figure from your Mortgage Broker, and your Title/Escrow Officer - ask them for a general estimate for now.*

3) <u>Property Inspection Costs</u> - (Example $500)

You never want to buy a property without professional physical inspections - this will absolutely include a general inspection, but depending on issues the initial general inspection may find, you may want a deeper, separate specialized inspection on a potential problem area such as plumbing, electrical, or AC/Heater, termite, etc. So, while you may not need it all, leaving a nice chunk in this line item as an estimate will serve you well. Your Realtor is going to guide you on inspections so I won't spend too much time on them here.

You may even want to travel to inspect the property yourself, and those costs can either go in this line as well, or, if you're like us, you may just consider those costs as part of your general education.

4) <u>Repair and Prep Costs</u> - (Example $1,500)

Once you have your home inspection, you will know every little thing that might need repairing. If any major issues are discovered, you and your Realtor can discuss whether you use those newly-discovered major repairs to negotiate on price, or as a reason to simply walk away. For now, let's assume your inspector only found minor issues – which is typically the case.

In addition, your property manager is going to assess the property and tell you what small improvements may be needed to make the property more rentable (perhaps tenants in that area will expect there to be a fridge included, etc.). For now, just put in an estimate of a couple thousand dollars so you don't get surprised later once you know all of the repairs/upgrades that are needed.

So, let's add up our Acquisition Costs:
(Purchase Price: $100,000)

20% Down Payment:	$20,000
Closing Costs:	$3,000
Inspection Costs:	$500
Repair/Prep Costs:	$1,500
Total:	**$25,000**

Another Acquisition "cost" (which is in quotes for a reason I will explain) is a reserve savings of about 6 months of your Mortgage Payment, Property Taxes and Insurance (which is referred to as "P-I-T-I"). This is a "cost" because while you do have to have this money in reserve, you don't actually spend it - you just have to flash it to your mortgage company so they feel comfortable that if you don't actually get a tenant in your property right away, you have at least 6 months of expenses in savings. Since you don't actually spend this money, I do not include it in the property analysis. Having a savings is a great idea anyway, so please don't sweat it – just know to expect it as a requirement. Again, your mortgage broker can tell you details such as perhaps this "reserve" can be in a retirement account, etc.

You also may be required to pre-pay insurance for the entire first year, or you may set up an "impound" account with your mortgage that builds in property taxes and insurance into your mortgage payment – but again – you will discuss all this with...yea – you get it...lol.   Even if some expenses are paid annually, we still want to express them as a monthly cost in our analysis to keep everything clear.

Again, keep in mind this is an initial analysis. When you are honing in on a particular property you will be able to refine all the numbers into exact, or near-exact figures. Maybe you don't need $1,500 for property prep – but then maybe insurance is double what you thought because your property is in a flood zone that nobody knew about – again, we're just getting a ballpark picture of the property at this stage of our analysis. There are a ton of variables that can make two similar houses very different once you run the numbers – which is why this is so critical to do!

2. Monthly Income:

The second group of numbers you need to know is all of the income you can expect from fully renting your proposed property. If this is a four-plex, you will have 4 numbers to gather here. If you are considering a single-family home, you will only need one number. And where do you get this number? Well, as a quick-and-dirty ballpark estimate, I don't mind either using a website like Rentometer.com or Zillow.com (or the Zillow phone-app) as described earlier - but as the transaction looks more serious, you will want to get an exact rental estimate from...guess who... yep - your property manager (who will have walked through the property with you and your Realtor before you even own the place).

So, let's add up our Monthly Income: (Example $1,000)

Rent, Unit 1:	$1,000
Rent, Unit 2:	$0
Rent, Unit 3:	$0
Rent, Unit 4:	$0
Total:	**$1,000**

3. Monthly Expenses:

The third, and final, group of numbers we need to gather together for our property analysis are the monthly expenses we will be facing - this will be the overhead we have in running our rental property as a business. They include some certain expenses as well as some possible expenses we want to prepare for. I will explain each one as we go:

1) <u>Mortgage Payment</u> - (Example $454.23)

Now, of course, your particular exact payment will be based on the interest rate you are getting at the moment which can be told to you by…. guess who! (Are you seeing a pattern here - you never have to come up with a number yourself as you fill out the numbers for analysis, the expert of that area on your team tells you everything).

But, to calculate a ballpark mortgage payment for now, you can use Excel, use a financial calculation tool, use a mortgage website, or even download a paper chart showing different payments at different balances and interest rates. Or, again, just email your Mortgage Broker to calculate it for you. For our example analysis, I'm running with a mortgage of $80,000 ($100,000 purchase price, minus your $20,000 down payment) with an interest rate of 5.5% per year, which comes to a monthly payment of $454.23.

2) <u>Property Management</u> - (Example 10% of Rent, or $100.00)

Almost universally, a property manager will charge 10% of the monthly rent as their management fee. So, on a $1,000 rental, their fee will be $100. Almost every manager will also charge you initially to "place" a new tenant in your property. This will range from half, to all, of your first month's rent with that new tenant, and it pays them for their costs in advertising the property, driving over countless times to show the property, running everybody's application (including credit and criminal background checks), etc.

For our analysis, let's only focus on the monthly management fee of 10%. This is because you and your team have determined that your property should be in demand to be rented most of the time – or you aren't going to buy it anyway, right? So, these tenant "turnover" costs should be very infrequent, and we are going to be factoring in something called "vacancy" here in a minute anyway (hold that thought).

3) Insurance - (Example $70.00)

Insurance coverages and costs for a rental property will be different than for a home you are going to live in yourself. That is why it is so important to have an investor-minded insurance agent on your team. Typically, you will need a "landlord policy" as opposed to a "homeowner policy" which will differ in that a landlord policy is concerned with insuring the property *itself*, but not necessarily any personal items *inside* it which belong to your tenant, (and can be covered with inexpensive "renter's insurance" your tenant can choose to get on their own).

Additionally, a landlord policy will include coverages for liability, in case anyone slips and hurts themselves on your property for example, and also coverages for loss of income if a fire, or other insured event, causes your property to not be rentable during the time repairs are being done.

You can ask your real estate agent, property manager, or mortgage broker for a referral to a local insurance agent, or, if you currently have insurance on your own home, or car, etc. with a national insurance company, you can always start there to see if you can add-on a landlord policy into your current insurance bundle. Personally, we are insured across the board with Safeco., a division of Liberty Mutual, and they have been wonderful and affordable, but this is just our experience, you will need to do your own local research.

Ask your insurance agent for some general ballpark cost estimates for insurance that you can plug into your analysis for now - and then as a specific property gets more real as a possible purchase, have your agent run a specific quote for that particular property so you can have an exact figure. At that same time your agent can check if your property requires any special supplemental insurance coverage because it is designated to be in a high-risk area (fire, flood, etc. as they will explain), which can greatly change the math on your analysis.

Note: While we generally look at insurance as a monthly expense for the sake of analysis, in reality you might pay your premium annually. If that's the case, you still want to create a monthly cost for your analysis numbers, because essentially this is the money you will have to set aside every month to pay your premium when it comes due. This is the same for Property Taxes... Hey, speaking of which...

4) Property Taxes - (Example $70.83)

Property Taxes in the area of your potential property should be easy to determine from your Title/Escrow Officer. Your Realtor undoubtedly has an Escrow Officer they already deal with. Simply ask your Realtor to introduce you (even by email), and then reach out to them. Ask them about anticipated Closing Costs (mentioned before) as well as typical Taxes both for this property, but also to use for estimate guidelines in general.

Typically, property taxes are based as a percentage of the value of the home, and the percentage will be the same for all homes in a particular area. So, use a general rate for the area on your analysis, then, as always, when a particular property gets more serious as a candidate for your purchase, have your Escrow Officer give you an exact figure to plug in.

Lastly, as with Insurance, you may not pay Property Tax every month, but you should factor in a "monthly set-aside" so that you have the cash on hand when an annual, or semi-annual bill comes due. It is that monthly set-aside number you want to put in your analysis.

5) <u>Vacancy</u> - (Example $50.00)

What's Vacancy? Vacancy is an estimated number you want to deduct as an "expense" in your analysis to represent the portion of the year you won't have a tenant in your property. Every area has its own "vacancy rate" or "vacancy factor" that can be calculated by your property manager - but any area that gets your team's "ok" as a purchase for you shouldn't have a vacancy rate of more than 5% or so. That means, 5% of the time, you are going to be prepping the property for a new tenant, because your old tenant has moved out. 5% of a year is a little over half a month. So, about half a month per year your property might be empty, and so we want to factor that in as a "cost" into our analysis.

Factoring in the reality of less-than-perfect outcomes in rental properties is to me what separates true professional investors from frantic, first-time amateurs.

Have a professional mindset starting now. Your rental isn't going to be rented every minute you own it. It might take several weeks to find the right tenant, and then that tenant might stay for 6 months – or many, many years! It's all in the cards - so have a professional-investor's mentality up front and you will avoid a lot of the panic and heartache that amateurs bring upon themselves by not embracing reality.

So, to analyze Vacancy – take what you expect in rent over the entire year (by taking your estimated monthly rental income and multiplying by 12). Take that annual number and multiply it again by 5% (0.05). And put that number in as a Vacancy "expense" (even though it's really not an expense - it's simply a lack of income - but I think you know what I mean).

For example: in the case of a $1,000 monthly rental rate, a 5% vacancy factor would be $50 a month.

Quick side-note – if you are hanging with me here as we go through these expenses I am very proud of you – this is the thought that pro's do that amateurs do not – and it will separate you from the pack as you hear "horror stories" from the accidental/amateur landlords in your life.

Ok, moving on…

6) <u>Repairs / Repair-Reserve</u> - (Example $50.00)

Like Vacancy previously, Repairs are something that professional investors know to set-aside money for, and factor them into their analysis before determining if a property is going to be profitable.

Now, keep in mind, all major repairs or prep-items have been identified at this point by your home inspector, and your property manager – and anything major the property needs will be accounted for (or you will pass on the property!). So, on day 1 when you get the keys, you are dealing with a property either already in darn good shape, ready for a tenant, or with minor prep to do you have already accounted the cost for. Still, we want to start saving up for the unexpected, but inevitable, repairs that will occur in the future as your tenant enjoys the property.

The reality is that your property, like every property, is eventually going to need something fixed. It might be nothing for a year and then suddenly a toilet starts leaking. It might be nothing for 5 years and then a water heater needs replacing. Or, it might be a clogged drain a month from now nobody could have expected. Whatever it is, large or small, we need to factor these repairs into our budget so we are never caught by surprise.

For extra peace of mind during your first year of ownership, a good real estate agent will always negotiate for the seller you are purchasing the property from to pay for a Home Warranty for the first year when we purchase a property. A Home Warranty is not a personal guarantee from the seller – it is an actual Warranty Policy from a major home warranty/insurance company! Yes, these exist, and it's a great thing to give you peace of mind mind that anything major (air conditioning, heating, etc.) that goes bad will be covered by this warranty.

Getting back to the topic of repairs - I like to set aside at least $50 a month per unit in my calculations for potential repairs. This is $600 a year. I'm comfortable that this is enough to cover small repairs that might happen soon, and/or save up for larger repairs that might happen later. If, however, you feel better setting aside $100, then do so! Sleeping at night and being more conservative is never a bad idea - just don't scare yourself out of what is really a great deal staring at you. Houses are rugged things built to last 100 years – literally. The "moving parts" that wear out in a house are well-known and can be prepared for. Your inspection will tell you the estimated usable life of major systems – so you should have years of advanced notice during which you can prepare and save up – or, when the time does come for a new roof, heater, etc. do you even want to pay cash for it from savings? Or, if your rent has increased along the way with the market, why not finance the needed upgrade and let your current tenant's higher rent cover the difference? You will know when you get there, for now, let's just set something aside.

Now, you might be thinking "Forget setting aside 50 bucks, I can get a 10-cent washer and fix a leaky faucet myself!" Um, excuse me - no you won't. You are a professional investor, not an amateur landlord - and maybe you even live in another state! Your property manager is going to handle every repair with his or her handyman he has a preferred relationship with so that your repairs are cost effective. Our property manager has a full-time handyman on staff, and so when a minor repair pops up we are only charged to reimburse the cost of his salary for that time he's helping us – plus any parts he had to buy for the repair. There's no way you can beat this deal doing a repair yourself or frantically finding a handyman out of the phone book.

Personally, we don't even know about small repairs our tenants call our property manager about until they are done and they appear on our Property Owner's Statement at the end of the month - how nice is that! Recently, we became aware that our tenant needed a plumber on Christmas Eve! That sounds like a cliché example out of a movie, but it really happened! Of course, we didn't even know until the middle of January. Again, contrast this experience with an amateur landlord getting a call himself from his own tenant to come spend their evening fixing a toilet – or calling for a plumber that will still answer the phone after-hours…barf!

7) Owner-Paid Utilities - *(If Applicable)*

If you are looking at purchasing a single-family home, this line item cost may not pertain to you (one of the advantages of a single-family property). But, if you are considering a multi-unit property, you are going to want to put a line-item in your expenses for Owner-Paid Utilities. This is because it is entirely likely that not all of the utilities are separately metered for each tenant.

Classically, it is common to see electric separately metered, but water and gas may not be. Or, lawn care/snow-removal, or trash service isn't something that could be separately billed to your tenants as they are considered common areas or common services. So, if any of this applies to you as the owner of your property, you will want to put a healthy estimate for these costs in your analysis.

Of course, the ultimate word on the exact figures would be for your Realtor to get an expense breakdown from the seller. Then you will see exactly what the current owner is paying each month. Expect costs to vary based on time of year, so be sure to see the entire year's expenses prior to a purchase. A summer gas bill is not going to be anything close to a winter gas bill - and you want to be prepared. So, add up the entire cost of a utility or service for the entire year and then divide that cost by 12 to find a monthly average to use in your analysis.

Special Notes: If a property looks like a winner to you except for exceptionally-high owner-paid utilities, this might be a reason to walk away from a deal, or it may be an opportunity for you if you are a bit more adventurous. For example, if a huge common gas bill for heating in winter is what is clobbering the numbers, call the local gas company and ask how big of a deal it might be to separately meter the gas? Call a plumber and get their estimate on the work needed that the Gas Company won't do, etc.

After getting these numbers you may find that it's all a big mess that you will never solve - or you may find that for a few thousand dollars, you can separately meter a property's gas or water - and now suddenly (as current leases expire and/or new tenants cycle in) a huge expense can be lifted from you as the owner and fairly passed along to the new tenants, which can make a huge impact on your cash-flow. If, however, just reading this idea stresses you out - stick with a single-family property for your first acquisition and you won't have to worry about any of this owner-paid utility stuff at all!

8) <u>Home-Owner Association (HOA) Fees</u> – *(If Applicable)*

HOA fees are mostly associated with Condo's, but you may be looking at a single-family home that is part of a Planned Urban Development (PUD)– meaning, while it feels like a normal "neighborhood" – the parks and amenities are actually maintained privately. I'm not a huge fan of Condo's as rentals, and PUD's are going to be the exception, not the rule, but just be aware that this does exist out there in case it happens to apply to your target property. If so, definitely have your Realtor investigate exactly what possible restrictions there may be on using your prospective property as a rental, and factor in the monthly "association dues" into your expense analysis.

Ok, so now let's add up our Monthly Expenses:

Mortgage Payment:	$454.23
Property Management:	$100
Insurance:	$70
Property Taxes:	$70.83
Vacancy:	$50
Repairs:	$50
Owner-Paid Utilities:	$0
HOA/PUD Dues	$0
Total:	**$795.06**

Determining Monthly Cash-Flow:

Now we have the three sets of numbers we will need for an analysis: our acquisition costs, our monthly income, and our monthly expenses – so now let's put them all together and see what we've got! Start with your monthly income and subtract your monthly expenses. The amount left is called your *Monthly Cash Flow.* In our example:

Monthly Income:	$1,000
Minus:	
Monthly Expenses:	$795.06
Monthly Cash Flow:	**$204.94**

Now, hopefully your monthly cash flow is a positive number! Of course, if you are left with a negative number, you are dealing with negative cash flow! Yikes! But, however it turns out - you just quickly gave yourself the reality of the deal before deciding to move forward - and that is powerful.

So, now we see your monthly cash flow in terms of raw dollars. But, what do these dollars represent in terms of your percentage Return-On-Investment (ROI)? ROI takes different forms, so let's go through them step-by-step, beginning with the most important, which is called the Cash-On-Cash Return.

Cash-On-Cash Return:

The first ROI number we want to determine is what is known as a Cash-On-Cash Return. A Cash-On-Cash-Return (COCR) is literally all the cash you had to put in, vs. all of the cash you are able to take out - over a year. This number tells you how strong of a cash-flowing investment the property is, without factoring in any other source of income or benefit. Calculating COCR is a very powerful analysis to do, because it literally tells you what income you are effectively about to "purchase" when you acquire this property. This should be clear as we run through an example.

To begin, let's put all of the numbers back up on the board for us to look at as we begin to calculate our Cash-On-Cash Return.

Acquisition Costs:

20% Down Payment:	$20,000
Closing Costs:	$3,000
Inspection Costs:	$500
Repair & Prep Costs:	$1,500
Total:	**$25,000**

Monthly Income:

Rent, Unit 1:	$1,000
Rent, Unit 2:	$0
Rent, Unit 3:	$0
Rent, Unit 4:	$0
Total:	**$1,000**

Monthly Expenses:

Mortgage Payment:	$454.23
Property Management:	$100
Insurance:	$70
Property Taxes:	$70.83
Vacancy:	$50
Repairs:	$50
Owner-Paid Utilities:	$0
HOA/PUD	$0
Total:	**$795.06**

Monthly Cash Flow:

Monthly Income:	$1,000
Minus:	
Monthly Expenses:	$795.06
Cash Flow:	**$204.94**

To determine your Cash-On-Cash Return:

Step 1: Take your Monthly Cash Flow number and multiply it by 12, which will give you your Annual Cash Flow.

Example:	Monthly Cash Flow:	$204.94
		x12
	Annual Cash Flow:	**$2,459.23**

Step 2: Take your Annual Cash Flow, and Divide it by your Total Acquisition Costs.

Example: Annual Cash Flow: $2,459.23
divided by
Acquisition Costs: $25,000
Result: **0.0984**

Step 3: Take the result of your division, and move the decimal point over to the right by 2 spaces. That is your Cash-On-Cash Return expressed as a percentage.

Example: 0.0984 = **9.84%**

So, what you are looking at is the percentage that all the cash you put in to purchase the property is creating you in terms of spendable cash profit each year. In our example, you have put $25,000 cash *into* an investment that is producing you $2,459.23 of new cash *out* over the first year. In this case, it means that 9.84% of the cash you put in is being produced back for you each year.

A Cash-on-Cash return is the most important number in rental real estate analysis.

The cash-on-cash return represents actual, spendable cash being produced, and it does not require any speculation in terms of whether the property will go up in value over time. As the years go by, will the rents increase in your area? Will your property value appreciate over time? None of this speculation is used in the cash-on-cash analysis – only known, current, factual numbers. That's why I love it.

If you're an Excel junkie like me, you can put all of the analysis I just took you though in one easy column like I have on the next page. *Note: I am working on a user-friendly "plug in the numbers" version of this Excel file. When I have it ready, I am happy to email to you for free. Simply drop me an email to request it (and/or introduce yourself) to: ElhardtRealEstate@Gmail.com*

RENTAL PROPERTY ANALYZER
123 Main St. Anywhere, USA 90210

ACQUISITION COSTS

Purchase Price	**$100,000.00**
20% Down-Payment	**$20,000.00**
First Mortgage	$80,000.00
30-yr, 5.5% Fixed Payment	($454.23)
Inspection Costs	$500.00
Repair/Prep Costs	$1,500.00
Closing Costs (3.0% Est)	$3,000.00
Total Move-In Cash Needed:	**$25,000.00**

MONTHLY EXPENSES:

1st Mortgage Payment	$454.23
Home-Owners Association Fee	$0.00
Owner Utilities	$0.00
5% Vacancy	$50.00
Property Tax *(Estimate of 0.85%)*	$70.83
Repairs to Save in Reserve	$50.00
Property Insurance	$70.00
Property Management	$100.00
Total Monthly Expenses:	**$795.06**

MONTHLY RENTAL INCOME:

Rental Unit 1	$1,000
Rental Unit 2	$0
Rental Unit 3	$0
Rental Unit 4	$0
Total Income:	**$1,000**

INVESTMENT PERFORMANCE:

Monthly Cash-Flow	**$204.94**
x12 (Annual)	$2,459.23
Cash-on-Cash Return - Year 1	**9.84%**

THE ELHARDT FAMILY GUIDE TO YOUR FIRST RENTAL PROPERTY

The Internal Rate of Return

The Cash-On-Cash Return, while being the most important number to know, is not the whole story. That is because cash flow is not the only source of profit in a rental property. There are other, less visible sources of profit at play, as we mentioned way back at the beginning, which are: 1) Property Appreciation, and 2) Mortgage Pay-Down Equity Creation. When you factor in these elements, you are calculating what is called the Internal Rate of Return.

I don't like to rely on potential Property Appreciation in my analysis, because if it happens, it will happen on its own schedule, and it is not something I can control or expect. On the other hand, when it comes to Mortgage Pay-Down/Equity Creation, this is something that most definitely will happen, and precisely on a schedule – called an Amortization Schedule. Here's what I mean:

A little while ago when we were calculating our monthly expenses, one of the first expenses I had you list was your mortgage payment. Well, let's take a closer look at this mortgage payment, and you'll quickly see why it's a silent, second source of profit to you.

Every mortgage payment is a combination of interest, and principal. Meaning, some of your payment is actually paying down your loan, and some of your payment is simply interest paid for using the money. In the first years of a mortgage, most of every payment goes to interest. But, every time you make a payment, a little of your mortgage balance (called "principal") gets paid off. So, for the very next payment, since you had paid off a little bit of your principal in your last payment, a little more of the next payment goes to principal, and so on, and so on. This process is called *Amortization*.

So, in other words, while the mortgage payment you are making every month remains the same, where that payment gets divided into keeps leaning more and more toward principal, not interest. In the beginning, most of your payment is going to interest, but eventually, most of your payment is going to principal, until, one day 30 years later (or whatever your loan term is), poof, your property has been paid off!

A typical 30-year mortgage actually has 360 monthly payments, and, while the mortgage payment remains constant, each payment has a slightly different balance of principal and interest being credited for that payment.

In the example rental property we've been running with, ($100,000 property with a 20% down payment,) we are carrying a $80,000 mortgage. Here is a snapshot of an Amortization Schedule of the first 12 payments of a $80,000 mortgage at an example 5.5% interest rate:

Amortization Schedule

No	Amount	Interest	Principal	Balance
1	454.23	366.67	87.56	79,912.44
2	454.23	366.27	87.96	79,824.47
3	454.23	365.86	88.37	79,736.10
4	454.23	365.46	88.77	79,647.33
5	454.23	365.05	89.18	79,558.15
6	454.23	364.64	89.59	79,468.56
7	454.23	364.23	90.00	79,378.56
8	454.23	363.82	90.41	79,288.15
9	454.23	363.40	90.83	79,197.33
10	454.23	362.99	91.24	79,106.08
11	454.23	362.57	91.66	79,014.42
12	454.23	362.15	92.08	78,922.34

So, we can see that a 30-year Mortgage payment would be $454.23, but, to start out, the $454.23 itself would be broken down like this:

Principal: $87.56
Interest: $366.67
Total: **$454.23**

As you can see on the Amortization Schedule, while the total monthly payment always stays the same, as each payment is made, the next payment then has a slightly different mix of principal and interest. Don't drive yourself crazy with the pennies right now – just get a general average sense of the principal/interest breakdown over the first year and add it up. Looking at this example it seems that more or less $90 a month of loan principal is being paid off each month. *(For the snapshot above, I used a free phone app called "EZ Calculators," but a simple Google search can bring up other free online amortization calculators).*

So where does your internal "profit" come from here? Well, with every mortgage payment, the portion of the payment which is principal is going toward paying off your mortgage balance and thus, it is creating equity for you in your property. Yes, you may have vacancy from time to time, but the vast majority of your mortgage payments will be made from rental income – and, since mortgage payments happen no matter what, literally on a schedule, including them in an investment analysis is not speculation the way property appreciation is.

While mortgage balance pay-down isn't cash-flow you can easily access and spend today, it is legitimate "internal profit" being created for you that you can access one day when you refinance the property, sell the property, or simply enjoy the property forever once it's paid off - paid off by your tenants!

So, in our example analysis, your tenant – through the mortgage payments you are going to be making with their rental income - is going to be paying about $90 of your mortgage off each month over the first year. That adds up to $1,080 of equity created for you. In other words, after a year of payments, your original $80,000 mortgage has been paid down to a balance of about $78,900. Again, don't worry about all the pennies here. Let's add this $1,080 mortgage pay-down number into the overall income analysis and then calculate the total Internal Rate of Return:

Annual Cash Flow (As determined earlier):	$2,459.23
Mortgage Pay-Down Equity Created:	$1,080
Total First Year Profit, All Sources:	**$3,539.23**

Now, divide your profit from all sources: $3,539.23 by your Acquisition Costs of $25,000, and your total Internal Rate of Return is: **14.2%**

Yikes! Over 14% - That's awesome!

Sorry, I couldn't hold back my excitement – if you're not sharing in it, let me review what we've just achieved…

We are talking about a "whatever" 3-bedroom house, in a "whatever" neighborhood that is as boring as it gets. We are *not* using any speculation in our analysis, and only using real rental rates in the area, real mortgage rates, real insurance rates, real property management rates, etc.

But we *are* assuming some things will go wrong! We are assuming things will break, and the property will experience some time without a tenant in it. We are even factoring in hundreds of dollars of paint, carpet, or other prep to even get the property ready for its first tenant. In other words, these numbers are very realistic, if not conservative - and we are cracking a 14% return?

Where else can you go and produce such a high return with a *conservative* investment? Remember - Mutual Funds brag about 10-12% "average" returns for aggressive investments over the "long term" (decades) after many good and bad – unpredictable years are all mixed together. Mutual Funds would prepare you that returns on a "conservative" investment would be closer to 4 or 5%. Banks take out freaking billboards bragging about their CD (Certificate of Deposit) rates when they can be over 2%!

Yet, here is your "boring" single family home (or duplex, etc.) – and you are crushing 14%? Seriously? But, you may have different expectations, so let's take a closer look at the topic of returns…

Chapter 15:

What Kind of Return Can I Expect?

As I have seen by very frequently analyzing deals myself, and I have also heard from fellow investors, total returns of 10% to 15% per year - and even higher, are very common in properly-selected rental real estate.

For our purposes, we like seeing Cash-On-Cash Returns near or over 10% ("double-digit"), then I want to see Internal Rates of Return in the strong 15% range or better... But - again, a lot depends on you and your preferences as an investor, as I will explain:

You might be more comfortable paying a little more for a property to be in a solid B-plus area, have a little more stable tenant pool, and maybe get a little "less" of a return - which to me would be Cash-On-Cash Return of maybe 7% or 8%, and a total, Internal Rate of Return of $11% or 12%. Then, as the years go by, your mortgage payment will remain stable while your rents may likely increase, so in effect you will "grow into" a better return over time.

Or, you might be more than comfortable in a more working-class C-Area that does a little better than the 1% Rule used in the last chapter's example. Wherever your investor's "gut" leads you, always keep your analysis estimates conservative – factor in vacancy and repairs, and if you get lucky and that year you don't have either – then that's a bonus! But always factor them in.

All I can say from my own experience, and from listening to other professional investors, is that double-digit total returns are not that hard to expect. All the while, you are investing in boring, reliable, and even "cute" houses in stable neighborhoods. You also have an asset bolted to Planet Earth you can go tap on with your knuckles.

Officially being redundant now, I must contrast this once again briefly with the traditional world of 401(k)'s, Mutual Funds, Annuities, Etc. which classifies you as either a "Conservative" or "Aggressive" investor based on how much "Risk" you are willing to take on. Then they tell you that you need to take on higher risk to expect higher reward. Then they will explain that based on your "Risk Tolerance" you can expect long-term average returns on your money of anywhere from 1% - 12%

You are even given a "risk tolerance test" to see what kind of investor you are! If you actually want to avoid high-risk investing you have to answer "yes" to test questions like *"I am willing to accept much lower returns in exchange for experiencing less risk."* Based on your answers you are given a Risk Tolerance Score, and then your advisor is obligated to only put you in investments that are approved based on your score.

What crap.

That's why I don't sell that stuff anymore. You can get a cute, boring rental house that blows away the returns of an "aggressive" mutual fund all day every day. You will know all of the costs up front, you will know all of the rent we can expect in that area up front, you will have the house inspected, you will have a home warranty, you also have it insured. That's about as non-risky as it gets in my book, which is why a little old no-nonsense church-lady like my Aunt Laura found it so appealing and do-able.

For such a safe, secure investment, the traditional investing world would likely offer 1-2% interest per year, with "aggressive risk" sign-your-life-away, please-don't-sue-us investments getting 12%

So, what if your first property you are comfortable with only produced 5-8%, but it did so regardless of what the stock market was doing... and it did so forever and ever and eventually our grandchildren owned it? Compare that to the massive catastrophe of a bad year in the stock market, and there *is* no comparison.

Again – remember the purpose of your first rental property. For us, we looked at our first rental as a fun adventure / learning experience we would be willing to pay tuition for if it was a class – except that it was happening in real life with a profitable investment waiting in the end.

So, with that in mind, maybe you do travel a bit more on your first deal than you will on your next ones, because it is on this first deal where you will be building a team and getting acquainted with a new area. So, if a flight or two has to go on some credit cards – I consider that tuition. Anything regarding the hard costs of the property purchase, however, is what needs to be analyzed in determining the quality of the deal.

Chapter 16:

Making a Decision

So, my friend, you have researched a city, researched a neighborhood, you have found a property, you have run the numbers, you have the blessing of your team, and so now what.... I will tell you this - your analysis will only take you so far. Your "gut" will have to take you a bit further, and then you will simply have to take a leap of action, and faith in the process.

Run the numbers, and then run all of your fears and concerns past your property manager. Get all of your "what if's" address, and at this point your head should be as comfortable as it can be.

Now, let's get your heart comfortable as it can be too: Put the numbers aside and just ask yourself - can you see someone wanting to live in the property? Maybe it's not your favorite color but can you see the rentable utility in it as a home? Can you see someone out there really liking it? If so – there's your answer.

Remind yourself that this is not your last rental property - it is your first. Remind yourself that you might own this property for generations. Get out of your own head and ask yourself if at the end of the day it all "feels" right.

And if it does, say a prayer, propose a toast - and pull the trigger.

PART 6

RUNNING A
RENTAL PROPERTY BUSINESS

Chapter 17:

Getting it Rented

This is a perfect time to pause and reflect on just how wonderful it is to have a team of experts you direct. Let's review...

Your Realtor –
helped you find the property.

Your Mortgage Broker –
helped you find the money to purchase the property.

Your Property Manager –
helped you assess the rentability of the property.

Your Property Inspector –
told you anything wrong with the property.

Your Insurance Agent –
got you the coverage you need as an investor.

Your Title / Escrow Company –
made sure the property transaction closed.

...and here you are with the keys!   So, let's get this sucker rented!

Your property manager takes center stage at this step. Your property manager already assessed and discussed with you what work is needed to prep the property for rental, so now it's time to get it done! Your manager will know the best handymen and/or suppliers to get all of the prep handled.

Depending on the area, maybe tenants expect there to be a fridge, maybe you need to paint a wall, or shampoo the carpets. Again, your manager will know and will guide you. Your manager is also going to start immediately marketing the property for rental. At this point, follow their lead. Your manager will notify you as rental applications come in from possible tenants, at which point, follow their advice and discuss why they like certain applicants over others. Before you know it, there will be a tenant living in your property!

Remember, once your property is rented, your education really begins at this stage! You will be getting used to working with your manager - you will have the thrill of getting statements every month showing the income from the tenant, as well as what expenses were deducted and why.

Since your tenant is paying rent to your manager directly - all expenses relating to their management fee and any repairs for that month will be deducted from the rent by your manager prior to your manager dispersing funds to you - which is wonderful. In our case - we have such a great relationship with our manager we usually don't hear about problems until they are solved. A toilet leaked, a fuse burned out, no big deal. Our manager does not call us for this stuff - they just take care of it at reasonable cost with their in-house handyman or preferred service provider.

After a few months you will be very used to your new status as an investor. You will be getting statements each month that report to you how your investment is operating from a financial standpoint.

On the following page is a partial sample of what one of our manager's Monthly Owner's Statements look like, giving a running total of where things stand at any given time. I purposefully chose this segment as an example because it is from a month where something went "wrong" on this property. Oh no! But look at how it was handled...quickly and inexpensively, and without bothering us.

Again, my wife and I literally find out about most minor problems after they have already been solved (for larger strategic decisions regarding the property, however, such as a new tenant placement, our manager calls us right away).

Description	Income	Expense	Balance
Beginning Cash Balance as of 02/19/2019			350.00
Rent Income - March 2019	895.00		1,245.00
Management fees - Management fees for 03/2019		89.50	1,155.50
Electricity - Tenant called about broken switch. Trouble shoot and repair. - Tenant called about broken switch. Trouble shoot and repair.		60.00	1,095.50
Owner Distribution - Owner payment for 03/2019		745.50	350.00
Ending Cash Balance			350.00
	895.00	895.00	

Most months, no repairs are deducted – which isn't "luck" – it's to be expected when you purchase a property following our system – which includes getting a property inspection, and fixing anything up-front that might be an issue, and giving you an estimate of the "usable life" left of other major systems of the house so you can be sure of how to prepare. Remember, our Realtor even negotiated a Home Warranty for us as part of the deal in case anything major went out unexpectedly the first year.

Sure, "one day," many years from now, your property will eventually need a new roof, or other major system. But by then, many years should have passed. When that time comes, reassess where you stand with the property. Maybe you finance a new roof, and that creates a $90 a month payment that is easily covered by the market rent increases you've been able to make on the property. Whatever the situation at the time, the process of analysis is the same – use your investor's eye to look at the property's equity and cash-flow at that time and the right solution will present itself in your mind.

Aside from issues with the physical property, there will also be people-related bumps along the way. For example, if you have a great tenant for over a year and then suddenly they have to be late with rent one month – don't panic! Get the whole story.

This happened to us, and it turned out that they had cashed their paycheck and then got robbed at a gas station – they simply didn't have the money! So, what do you do? Enforce the rules strictly and slap them with a late fee? Or, get frustrated and say to yourself "why is anyone carrying cash anymore?"

What we chose to do waive the late fee – break their rent into payments they can catch up on over the next month, and then we asked our manager to give them a $100 gift card from Wal-Mart as a "hang in there" gift. Heck – we're just really giving back $100 of their own rent money anyway. Has a "landlord" ever done that for them? How many would? How do you think that made them feel?

Oh, Brian, you're so nice – but is this good business? YES! Tenants are your customers. If you have a proven, great customer and they are just having some life-issues happening – try working with them. If they move out, now you have to clean, paint, market the property, etc. Is all of that really worth a little compassion for a moment?

At the same time, hold your tenants to a standard – if you have a long-term tenant, as the years go by, raise the rent up to true market level, but be very responsive to their needs in return. Your property manager ran a thorough background check on your tenants up front, so you shouldn't expect any illegal activity, but if such nonsense arises let's say from their daughter's new boyfriend - deal with it accordingly. My point isn't to always be nice, or always be strict, but rather take each situation as it comes and really assess it as an investor in property – which is also an investment in people, and their lives. Again, your property manager will guide you.

What about every year or so, surprise them by having the carpets professionally cleaned for them – something that makes their living in the home nicer – and at the same time protects the life of the carpet for you as the investor. This is just an example – you and your property manager will of course use your own wisdom and instincts.

And, if you have a bad tenant – deal with them accordingly as well. Be fair. Be firm – but realize you will be likely be asking for your tenant's patience along the way as well – when a switch gives out and your handyman can't get there until tomorrow so they have to wash dishes in the dark for the night, etc. So, even if you never meet your tenants, build a great relationship – through your actions as an owner.

Chapter 18:

Money Management

At this point you have a rented, "stabilized" rental property that is a "performing asset" - meaning it is generating income. How do you manage this money properly? Here are a few steps to consider:

Separate Bank Account

You will want to strongly conned opening a special bank account just for your rental property. All income from your Property Manager gets direct-deposited into this account - and all expenses you have to pay each month like the mortgage, are paid from this account.

Depending on what kind of mortgage you have, you may have what is called an "Impound Account" attached to your mortgage that literally gathers your property taxes and insurance payments as a lump sum along with your mortgage payment. Or, you may pay your mortgage separately, and then pay your property taxes and insurance directly. Either way, having this bank account to work from is extremely helpful as you always know the money is there waiting for your planned expenses. Anything extra, assuming you don't need it to live on, can just sit there and add up - waiting for an emergency repair - or eventually a down payment on your next rental property.

Creating a Legal Entity

You may wish to speak to a Real Estate Attorney about the possibility of setting up an official "business entity," such as an LLC (Limited Liability Company) to run your investment as a real company - not just as a personal investment. This will be an exciting phase of your education as a real estate investor as you discuss this with your Attorney. (If you don't know a good real estate Attorney - you already have the skills of finding one through the referral skills you learned while building your team).

A legal entity literally takes title to your rental property - for example, our LLC is called Elhardt Real Estate, LLC - and it is what appears on title. Therefore, if we are sued as a business, or personally, one does not bleed into the other as easily than if we personally held title in our own personal names. Again, this is where a discussion with your attorney is a great idea, and most good ones give initial consultations for free. Your CPA will likely have a referral to a great attorney if you don't know of one, which leads me to...

Your CPA

Please keep in mind that you do not have to form a legal entity like an LLC to be in business - your rental property is a business right now! As such, you are entitled to every conceivable tax advantage allowed to rental investors. Do not miss out on these tremendous benefits by thinking you know it all - or by using the old tax person you've used for years before you were an investor.

Your tax return used to cost 50 bucks and it saved you nothing. As an investor, your tax return will cost you hundreds - and it will save you thousands. You need a real CPA (Certified Public Accountant) that also understands and specializes in business owners and/or real estate investors. If you are their smallest client (for now) then perfect - you won't out-grow them as you build your empire. But you need them now. Period.

Chapter 19:

Long-Term Planning

When a rental property is rented and making income every month, it is called a "Performing Asset." When you have a performing asset like a rental property, it doesn't just give you cash-flow now, it gives you a piece on your life's financial chess-board to make moves with in the future.

You have to stay mentally engaged as an owner. While rental real estate investing is a slow-paced, easy-to-grasp business, and you have likely delegated a lot of day-to-day tasks to your team, you are still the captain. You must "manage your manager." Your team is there to feed you accurate information, and execute your orders, but you have to remain the head of what you are doing and why. The three aspects of a property you will always have to measure are Equity, Rental Income, and Property Rentability.

Equity

Gaining equity in your property as the years go by is a good thing – but it does change the dynamics of your return on investment. The more equity you have, the more money you have "tied up" in this property to produce the rental income.

Rental Income

Keeping an eye on what current market rent has become as years go by will be critical in assessing whether to hold onto any particular property and should be monitored closely.

Property Rentability

Rentability is different than rent. Rentability is how desirable your particular property is in the area it is - now that some years have passed.

Having a firm grasp of Equity, Rental Income, and Rentability will give you the raw numbers to think with – but then you have to filter that raw data through your personal goals as an investor – and there is not necessarily a wrong answer!

For instance, after 10 years of successful operation, let's say you have some significant equity sitting in your property from the mortgage being paid down, and who knows, maybe even some appreciation in the market value of the property having risen. What do you want to do with that equity? Do you want to eventually pay off this property? Or, do you want to refinance the property, and pull back out all the cash you can – maybe paying to put on a new roof, give yourself a nice vacation, and perhaps using the rest for a down-payment on another rental property?

Or, do you have so much equity in this property relative to the rent it can command today, that it doesn't even make sense to own this particular piece of real estate anymore? Maybe the area has become less desirable and so the qualifications of your potential pool of tenants is getting worse. Or, maybe the area has been getting better and now after all of these years you will need to remodel the home to meet the expectations of the new, higher-qualified tenant pool. If these are the case, perhaps selling the property as-is and using all of the equity – which includes your original down-payment – over into a larger, or more expensive rental property elsewhere makes sense.

Or, a bit older in years yourself then, are you more excited about the idea of simply paying off the property you have had so long and know so well, even if it means you are locking up a lot of equity to do so – the simplicity of it all just appeals to you at that stage of your life, so you don't change a darn thing! Only you can decide at that time, and go with your investor's gut.

With tax advantages, such as a "1031 Exchange" your CPA can help you think through how to sell, refinance, pay-off, or even leave behind rental property as a legacy. Your job as an investor is to use the timeless, never-changing principals of analysis and team building as you navigate the timely, constantly-changing information such as the interest rates and tax laws of tomorrow.

Chapter 20:

Gut Check Time

I am so glad you have read the book this far, and have really given yourself a chance to see what it is going to take to become a rental real estate investor. At this point, take a moment and ask yourself which of the following statements describe how you are really feeling about investing in rental real estate:

Are you feeling:

1) Gung-ho to get started building your rental real estate business by yourself?

2) Excited about building a real estate business, but not quite sure if you trust yourself to do it alone and may want some help from a coach?

3) Still excited about the thought of owning rental real estate, but - coach or no coach - you do not see yourself ever wanting to take on the adventure of building a team and becoming an investor yourself?

If #1 describes you – then I truly wish you the best possible luck out there and please let me know about your experiences! I'm honored to have been part of what inspired your journey.

If #2 describes you – read on, because we are going to talk about working with a coach (which is the way I started) who will help you become your own, hands-on investor.

If #3 describes you – also read on, because we are also going to talk about available options to invest in rental real estate without actually personally becoming a hands-on investor.

Which road ahead is best for you really all boils down to one question – and there's no wrong answer – but it's important that you really know yourself and be honest. Deep down, do you really want to:

1) Simply own a real estate investment, or
2) Actually *be* a real estate investor.

It's the same thing as asking if you ultimately simply want to ride in an airplane as a passenger, or do you want to actually be a licensed pilot? You can experience much of the benefits of air-travel either way - I just don't want you to decide you just want to be a passenger out of fear or ignorance, because I really can teach you to fly a plane. But if being a passenger is the best fit for the "true you" then that's ok!

Think again of cooking and food - there are times in life when we pay to eat in a restaurant even though we know how to cook. It's more expensive, but it's convenient and if that's what makes our day work better today so you can focus on other things then that's great. Then paying more for a result is a strategic choice.

What I *don't* want to hear is that you are eating in restaurants your whole life because nobody taught you to cook. In the same way - if being a rental real estate investor is in your heart - let's find you a way up the mountain.

So, if you're not gung-ho to get started yourself, let's explore our options, and see what matches up with the true you of who you are today, and more importantly, who you are willing to become with the right help.

PART 7

INVESTING WITH HELP

Chapter 21:

Hiring a Coach

Let's say you don't want to be stuck having to eat in restaurants your whole life - but you're not confident to be your own cook just from a cookbook.

Well, if this is the case, what if an experienced chef could go with you to the grocery store, and then visit you at home and show you how to cook in your own kitchen? That would be pretty sweet. Well - real estate speaking, that is totally available to you.

But why would a successful investor want to "share their secrets" by coaching you? Here's reality – number one, there are no secrets when it comes to deal analysis and how to run a successful rental real estate business, it just might seem that way because there are so many "amateur landlords" out there that don't bother to learn them. Number two, even the richest real estate investor in the world can't even begin to do every deal that's available out there. There are literally millions of potential rental properties to be found, and thinking you are going to own them all is like thinking you are going to catch every fish in the ocean. It's insane.

What to look for in a Coach

A real estate coach is not there to simply teach you concepts you can find on Google – they are also not there to simply dictate to you what to do. A great coach is there to help you develop your own skills in how to apply investing knowledge so that you can learn to look at things through an investor's eye. A coach is there are there to help you hunt, help you analyze, help you build a team (or borrow theirs) so you personally gain the instincts and knowledge of an investor.

Think of a personal fitness trainer– they may show up with dumbbells and a lot of knowledge – but then their job is to personalize and help you apply the work of developing your own muscles. In the same way, a great real estate investing coach ultimately teaches you to not need them anymore - because you will have become the investor. In school, you are "cheating" if you pay someone for the answers on a test. In business, however, the smartest people that want to win the quickest are the ones that know to hire coaches first!

Years ago, on my first rental deal, I had a best-friend as a business partner, and together we hired a coach to teach us what they knew. This gave us the confidence to get out of our heads, trust our analysis, and make the first move. Aunt Laura also had a partner in her brother (my grandfather) Leonard. Even today I have a partner in my wife, who is fully engaged in every deal we do and who often provides the wisdom of what to pursue while I more provide the numbers behind it.

There are two ways you can fail – first is by not knowing how to do things right – the second is not trusting yourself to know what the right thing is! The latter is the most tragic, because you can actually be on your way to winning and not know it. Think of working out in a gym – doing it wrong, your muscles will be sore…and doing it *right* your muscles will be sore! But knowing a good sore that is building muscle vs. a bad sore that is leading to a trip to the hospital is what the coach is there to help you with.

Coaches are not cheap - but if you are planning on putting $20,000 - $30,000 into an investment, why not add a few hundred, or a few thousand more into your business plan and have the benefit of someone else's experience, and connections to "cheat off of?" This is by far the fastest road up the mountain. You will still be the investor - just like with a golf coach, you will still have to hit the ball - but you will have a huge advantage of knowing if you are on the right track or not. You will have homework to do, but you will have someone to check it that cares about you.

Finding a Coach

You can absolutely find real estate investing coaches out there, and I want you to find the best fit for you. But, I hope you don't mind I mention the fact that I could be your coach as well. This is by no means a sales pitch – this is simply for the reader that has really felt they have connected not just with the concepts and facts I've relayed in this book, but also to me, my personality, and style of teaching. (Even if I am truly not the best coach for you - the rest of this chapter will explain my coaching philosophy which should be helpful to you in what to look for in a coach).

I could rattle on about the investors I've worked for through the years and the sophisticated deal structures I've been a part of, and that might help sell intimidating advanced courses that sit on your shelf with the others. But that wouldn't be the power of having me as your coach for your first rental property.

The power would be in the fact that my wife and I have actually done all of the things we describe in this book: the flights to a new city to build our new team relationships, touring possible properties, doing the analysis of the numbers – and if we can become successful investors while working full-time, typical jobs, so we know it can be done. And – we've done so in recent years – we remember what it is like to be new. That's huge – because while most guru's sell you on the hundreds of rental properties they have, I'm selling you on the fact that we are still building our business in real time right now. But, we're off of square one - we've done it – we're up that first hill, and we're willing to stop and turn around, and help you get up at least to where we are. That first deal is where most people get stuck. We're past that – and we can help you get there.

Whatever coach you may select, let me impress upon you one concept to embrace…

Do not waste another dime "learning" how to do a deal – spend all future time and money actually doing a deal.

I cannot emphasize this enough. If you want to go skydiving, then go skydiving! If to make that possible, you hire a coach to "jump tandem" with you the first time or two – then so be it – then pay them to jump with you – but to spend thousands of dollars only on classroom instruction on skydiving concepts will never get you there.

If you would like to start a conversation about being coached by me personally, please email me at: elhardtrealestate@gmail.com

But, if you are thinking that - coach or no coach - you are never going to get out there, build a team, and actually find a rental property yourself, let's take a look at some other options…

Chapter 22:

"Turn-Key" Rental Properties?

I want to briefly talk about something just to get it out of the way. There are companies out there that are essentially house-flippers that buy run down houses, fix them up - and then right before they sell them they rent them out...and then sell them as rented rental properties to rental-property investors. They call these "Turn-Key" rental properties.

While this might sound very appealing - here is something to consider - and why I do not like this option for you as a first-time investor: In the world of investing, you either want to be a completely active, or a completely passive investor in any given investment. In other words, either you want to drive, or someone else should drive – but two people driving is a recipe for disaster.

For example, in a Mutual Fund, you, as the investor, are completely passive and hands-off. Yes, you made the choice to purchase the mutual fund and "get on the plane" so to speak, but after that you are merely a passenger and your job is to watch the movie while the pilot does the flying.

The "pilot" in the case of a Mutual Fund is a Fund Manager back on Wall Street managing your money along with all the other money in the fund. The fund manager puts in 80-hour work weeks stressing over the performance of the fund, which is tied to their annual bonus as well. You are completely passive - and you have a full-time professional literally making investment decisions for you at all times.

On the other hand - in a rental property, you are completely active and hands-on. Yes, you have a property manager for logistical support, but you researched and picked the city, the area, the property, the property manager, etc. You are the one that knows exactly what is going on and when to buy, sell, or adjust your investment. You are the pilot flying the plane. As a reward, you have control, and experience higher investment returns than being a mere passenger.

In the case of a turn-key rental property, however, you have the worst of both the passive and active worlds. You are ultimately responsible as the pilot flying the plane as the full-blown owner of the property (not merely a "shareholder") but you were only a passive "passenger" when the investment you own and are responsible for was being assembled for flight.

Someone else chose the property, remodeled it, someone else selected the area and neighborhood type. Someone else put a tenant in it, and then walked away and threw you the keys! People that buy these investments likely did nothing but look at the current cash-on-cash return numbers and say "yes" to the investment – without doing any other of the due diligence taught in this book to prepare you to be the owner of a successful rental property – a property that not only performs well, but that also truly suits you personally as an investor.

That's like a pilot getting a plane in the air and then saying - "here - you fly it." Holy crap! Maybe the property manager the turn-key company put in place for you is a great one - maybe the tenant in your property is great - maybe the neighborhood is great in reality, not just on paper – maybe, maybe, maybe. Yet, you hold all of the liability and responsibility of someone else's decisions? YIKES! Hell no.

The only way you could safely invest in a turn-key rental property is by being the active, hands-on investor doing your own analysis and due-diligence I describe in this book. If you want to do all of those steps before purchasing a turn-key rental, then you have my blessing! But, if you are willing and able to do all of that work yourself anyway...why do you need a turn-key rental in the first place?

Chapter 23:

Partner with an Experienced Investor

One alternative to being coached to cook, would be to cook with an experienced chef, but in their kitchen, not yours. This would involve actually partnering on a property with an experienced investor. If you have more money than time, and/or more time than experience, this could be a great alternative.

In partnering on a deal, you, as well as the experienced investor would both be "active" investors – you would absolutely be involved in decisions, but you would be bringing different elements to the table and it would be agreed upon up front who will be driving what functions of the deal.

Most commonly, the investor with more experience would be finding and analyzing the deal, would be bringing the team relationships, the due-diligence, etc. to assess the deal. That more experienced investor would also be leading the process in structuring the deal with the help of legal and tax counsel that would help all parties understand the arrangement. Then, you as the partner may bring in some, or all, of the cash, credit, or other financial strength to make the lender approve the "package" of the deal.

For this to really work effectively, the deal may have to be a little larger than a single-family home…. At a minimum, perhaps a duplex, triplex, or 4-plex, would work perhaps with two investors working together. Otherwise, an even larger deal such as an apartment complex would work with a handful of investors, or more. This process is called *Syndication* and can unlock investment opportunity for investors with various time, resources, and resources to contribute. Essentially, a new legal entity ("company") would be created specifically own and operate the property, each partner owning a share.

Of course, there would also have to be a great deal of agreement and alignment between you and the other investor in terms of what was expected. Still, it could be a great chance to have a front row seat while a real deal went down. Partnering is how I personally got so much experience in the beginning on my investing life myself as my friend's father financed a deal that my friend and I did the "leg-work" for. The knowledge and confidence I gained in that first deal is still fueling me today.

Finding a Partner

Finding a partner still starts with building a relationship, you can't get out of that! You can perhaps start attending some local investor's meet-up groups, or search online. If, however, you are curious about the possibility of partnering with us – yes! That is also an opportunity – but only if we really "click" and are the right fit.

What kind of deal would we Partner in?

Please know this is highly conceptual, and that any actual opportunity to partner together would have to be discussed directly. But, our Realtor relationships are always sending us deals that are larger than we can handle by ourselves at the moment, and those would be the deals we would be looking for partners on. In general, we would be looking at 5+ unit apartment complexes.

There's a lot of technical reasons why these larger deals make for much better partnering opportunities I would love to discuss with you. I'm very tempted to start explaining it here, but you already have a lot in your head by reading the book this far.

If you would like to discuss the possibility of partnering on a deal such as this, please email me at:

elhardtrealestate@gmail.com

Chapter 24:

Be a Private Lender

In the last chapter, we talked about partnering with an experienced investor on a larger deal. Partners are literally partial-owners, and their profit is of course based on the profit of the investment. However, if you would rather have a more-steady source of investment return that is truly "hands off," you may prefer to be a private lender instead.

Being a Private Lender means you would literally lend money to an experienced investor at a set interest rate - which that investor would then use to do deals with. Unlike a partner that would experience the ups and downs of a deal, you, as a lender, would receive a set payment at a set interest rate - typically many times the interest rate available at a bank, yet fully secured by the real estate being purchased by that investor. There may even be opportunities for bonus payments on top of the set interest rate.

Given the nature of the arrangement, you should receive many times the interest rate on your money than would be offered by any bank, yet with a loan secured by real property. To find lending opportunities you can do a Google search for "Hard Money Lenders" or "Private Lenders" in your area – and likely you will find lending companies looking to pair investors with private lenders like you.

Of course, if you would rather explore the possibility of being a lender with us - and be notified when such opportunities may arise, please email me at elhardtrealestate@gmail.com

Chapter 25:

Next Steps & Help for Your Journey

So, here we are at the end of the book.... The comfort-zone of "learning" is now over and the time to take action is here! I assure you that if you take the smallest action it will start unlocking a power and and momentum in you. Perhaps that means just going online and looking for some 1%-rule areas, or reaching out to a Realtor or Mortgage Broker and having a frank conversation about where you are. Whatever your next, small step in the process may be – do it now!

I'm also here to help as much as I can. I'm working on a more "user-friendly" version of my property analysis Excel sheet, if you would like to be on the list to be mailed a copy, just drop me an email at elhardtrealestate@gmail.com I'll also gladly keep you posted about YouTube videos and other free resources in the works. And please share your questions and your progress. I truly want to help.

Creating simple financial peace through rental real estate like Aunt Laura did isn't just an end in itself that should be reserved for real-estate fans. Rental property is a powerful source of passive income that can unlock your time and provide resources for other higher purposes God might have in mind for our lives. For that reason, I believe the freedom rental real estate can give is truly for everyone with a purpose...so, let's get that freedom for you!

Until then, peace,

Brian

AMDG

Notes: